The Art & Habits of Supernatural Success

The 12 Steps and Rules to Prosperity Leadership and Power

By: George Mentz

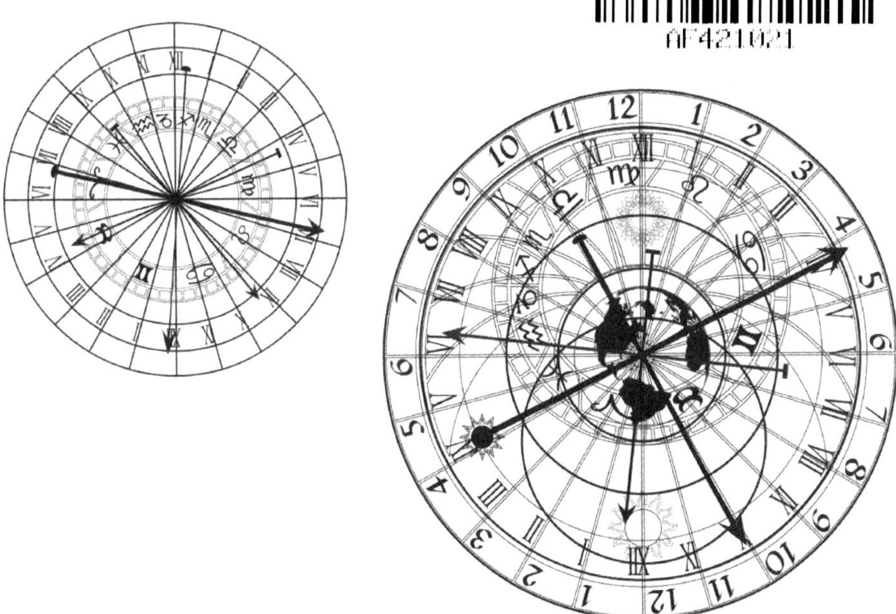

First published by
Mentzinger Media, LTD
http://www.gmentz.com
Endorsed by the Academy http://www.gafm.com
© George Mentz 2020

ISBN – Disclosed on Publishing
Library of Congress Cataloguing-in-Publication Data
Cataloguing in Publication Data
A catalogue record for this book is available online

Table of Contents

Summary of Ideas – A Parabolic Workbook to Success

Preface - After visiting and meeting with leaders in over 40 nations including executives, Kings, Ambassadors, Barons, Dukes, and Spiritual Leaders for various faiths, we have gathered some of the greatest insights to success, happiness, health and prosperity known to the world.

Introduction

Maximizing The Inner Power – The New Philosophy

I remember being at the Yale Club of New York City years ago researching philosophy and metaphysics and doing research at the nearby New York Library and the Yale Club Library.

While comparing many great gurus for the history of the world I came to a simple conclusion. From Buddha to Jesus, from Kant to Hegel, from Marcus Aurelius to Benjamin Franklin, the common denominator is subjective but the same and that is, "The great thinkers all seek peace of mind". Most wise folks know that with peace, you have a greater awareness, a clean running computer, less attachments, and the person "at peace" is free with expansive thinking and creativity.

As some point, all of us develop an internal hunger for a higher purpose and to master our destiny during our lives. This instinctive fire in the belly seemingly compels us to think and take action; we must change and adapt. Growth is necessary for the human condition. Finding a reason for being, where we can cultivate our talents and use them to improve life for ourselves and those we love, becomes vitally important. Striving for the personal best in ourselves while serving humanity is an ideal both important and noble. It is part of our desire for a greater good. Becoming the best we can be and doing the things we love to do in service and in leisure is a natural desire. This is true whether one is a righteous member if any religion or a follower of a philosophical practices, virtues, and ethics.   The state of Abundance is possible when we inherently understand the need to adapt, grow, and be prepared. You hold the golden key when you master your destiny by improving yourself in mind body and spirit.

This codex is a summary of the key philosophy and secrets needed to advance to your highest potential. If you need to learn even more to prepare yourself for this guide, we suggest several other authors: Marcus Aurelius, the gospels of Jesus Christ, Buddha, Pythagoras, Hegel, Kant, Emerson, von Goethe, Meister Eckhart, poetic Vedas and Eddas, the Book of Psalms, Zoroaster, Lao Tzu, Socrates, Plato, Aristotle, the Upanishads, and any great wisdom literature. Then, of course, we can seek more light from the authors in the bibliography.

One of the greatest secrets of mankind is that leaders and professionals have quietly used the philosophy contained herein for centuries. Keep this book close, use this secret technology, and master your destiny.

Whatever our vocation may be (e.g., mechanic or artist), you will need the right instruction and tools to gain excellence. The importance of natural expression is absolutely necessary for personal accomplishment and prosperity. Your highest form of expression requires an imaginative and resourceful life; it involves the abundance of ideas, things, and actions.

True and lasting prosperity has a spiritual foundation and balance. Genuine success is mastering excellence in body, mind, and spirit. When there is balance, ideas and energy naturally come from the universe to the person who is exercising this higher order of existence. When we are at our best and acting as effective individuals, we actually have more insights flowing to us from the universal source or consciousness of the infinite.

No let us focus firstly on the great philosophers of science and ethics. These great thinkers all contribute different ingredients to the recipe of a rich and fuller life. Read what each of them has to say, ponder their ideas, and then you will be ready to examine the rest of the book.

- Rene Descartes simplifies the essence of philosophy: "I think, therefore I am." With this statement, we must be able to find our being, or what people call their being-ness. The key is to reconnect your spirit and deeper-self with the universe in a way that is harmonious.

- George W. F. Hegel, a German philosopher, also believed that reality was absolute Spirit; we participate in our destinies and create our own realities.

- Meister Eckhart, the fourteenth-century Christian Neo-Platonist, personified the spiritual basics in these words: "If the only prayer you say in your life is 'Thank You,' that would suffice."

- Socrates said, "Know thyself," and, "The unexamined life is not worth living." Be willing to take a hard look at yourself in the mirror, and seek an honest appraisal of your character and behavior and let go.

- The French existentialist Jean-Paul Sartre was clear about accountability. We should start having responsibility for our actions going forward and refuse to be bogged down with self-victimization and blame. We must deal with the past.

- Ben Franklin, in his autobiography, used a process called the precept of order, where each day he took time to review his day, set goals, and see where he could improve his actions and character.

- Nietzsche said, "That which does not kill us makes us stronger," Thus, we need to face fear and get out of our comfort zones.

- Marcus Aurelius so eloquently said, "Take full account of the excellencies which you possess, and in gratitude remember how you would hanker after them, if you had them not." Aurelius includes another great quote that we should follow: "It is not death that a man should fear, but he should fear never beginning to live."

- Humanistic psychologists Carl Rogers and Abraham Maslow believed that people have an innate drive to be all they can be and to self-actualize. This intrinsic metaphysics plays a large role in facilitating the progression of the best in each of us.

- Aristotle's theory of potentiality: "Within each of us is a natural evolution toward fulfilling our potential."

- Immanuel Kant has implied that OUR Perception IS our reality. If you focus your thoughts on the best, then you will attract the best. Feed yourself with things that are good, learning about what is excellent, and these things will build your worldview and character.

- Dr. Carl Jung theorized that one finds their natural talents deep within the spirit of one's self. When we get in touch with our natural inclinations, it elevates our outward expression. It may not be easy, but if you act toward your higher purpose each day, the cosmic momentum will build to your advantage.

- Both Aristotle and Thomas Aquinas refer to God as the 'First Cause" or "Pure Mind." In essence, we come from this pure mind and first cause; we are created from the Source. We have desires and ideas flowing to us from a higher source at all times. What you do with your ideas and imagination is of extreme importance. Your ideas are yours, they are priceless, and they are consciously coming to you in every moment. Your creativity is your abundance

- The poet Johann Wolfgang von Goethe famously stated that "boldness is genius."

- Acclaimed self help author Robert Collier also believed that beginning any task created a nucleus of activity, bringing form from the formless. If you begin something and maintain faith in the process, you may then utilize the act of gratitude and praise which is like watering a flower with nourishment. In the same way a flower needs water, the universe craves peace, thanks, praise, and action, and the universe will respond accordingly with blessings.

- Engels and Marx believed firmly in productivity as the key to progress. The big metaphysical secret lies in becoming one with your desires, because you then become in tune with your objective! When we blend purpose and spirituality, our energy then becomes laser focused.

- The philosopher of existentialism Soren Kierkegaard was famous for saying, "We must think for ourselves and be suspicious of groupthink, and we should not worry about the ignorance of neighbors and society."

- Remember, Emerson, St. Augustine, and Plato believed that evil is not a diabolical force but rather the absence of good.

- Henry David Thoreau believed that we should put our "Conscience before conformity." Thus, your natural creativity and labor will be fun, and you will learn to freely accept premiums and rewards for your quality services and the products in relation to your craft.

- British political philosopher John Locke believed in a liberal, anti-authoritarian theory of the state. His practical theory of knowledge advocated religious toleration and personal identity. His philosophy suggests that order is necessary to protect the individual, and man is endowed with inalienable rights where these rights are gained through work and effort.

- Alfred Wallace, the founder of evolution theory with Darwin, systematically came to believe evolution was sometimes guided by a higher power and that evolution could not account for the evolution of consciousness.

- The nineteenth-century European philosopher Arthur Schopenhauer believed that we are motivated by our will, and it is our will that is our sense of reality. Therefore, willingness is at the core of our growth and advancement. Desire is good and comes from the Spirit. Seeing past the illusion of what seems apparent, and acting on healthy desires, is the key to growth and happiness.

Whether you are a student of Locke, Emerson, Ayn Rand, Ben Franklin, Frederick Douglas, or Buddha, there are some eternal truths. The great lesson from many of the world's legendary philosophers is that the individual is an important and unique part of the whole. Each person should master themselves; education, knowledge, and inner peace are essential. Efficient effort is vital for advancement. Growing in faith, knowingness, and wisdom are all important factors of duty to ourselves and to society. Your contributions may seem small, but your spiritual creativity and service may positively affect generations to come. Overall, the ripple effect of one pebble tossed in the lake has a broad impact on the whole of its contents.

The results of practicing these principles and suggestions will result in a natural expression of your life purpose that becomes a reality—you will become who you were meant to be. It may require great energy from you, but it will feel eventually like child's play. You may find many challenges, but the experience of life will be invigorating when you pause in those moments to stop and smell the roses. Life is delicate and sometimes short, and you may be compelled to dedicate energy to definitive ends. All mortals are faced with these timeless questions: What do you want to be remembered for? How do you want to impact the world? What is your potential legacy?

You have within you the power to connect to the universal force. This force is the creative and animating energy that permeates the universe. Like gravity or electricity, the Force is not seen, but exists as the all-pervading framework for which every law hinges upon. This interstellar force is also known as God or "The Life Force". This unlimited power is everywhere as creation is constant. New ideas, new art & music, new planets, new galaxies, new species, new worlds are continuously manifesting at this very moment.

That special part of your consciousness that can be in-tune with this force is referred to by the great teachers of metaphysics as the subjective mind or higher consciousness.

Directed thought-energy can be focused where the individual may act as a creative force within the universal framework.   This supernatural power is willing to serve you and grant you anything that you earnestly and sincerely desire with focus, action, heartfelt gratitude and emotion.

If Faith is the substance of things hoped for, then that very Substance can also be qualified as the energy of our attention and thoughts.   Belief and faith are the same in that they mean that we accept what is unseen.   Energy is consciousness, and thus, "thought awareness" is energy. All things created equally in perfect balance, the energy of faith, attention, and mind can tilt the cosmic balance of life, happiness, and success in our favor.

This is why spiritual-metaphysics is so important because the participant who engages mental-cooperation with universal law attains the ability to optimize: body, mind and spirit. The galactic framework of forces that we seek to cooperate with is what many call: "the Spirit of the Universe" and "the spirit within you".

All of us go through life with a steady stream of ideas, thoughts, and desires. Tapping into that greater, infinite-self expands our intuitive abilities to best use our priceless inspiration.   Thus, becoming aware that we may operate at a higher order of being is where achievement truly begins, and then, we become willing to take the actions that provide results. Co-operation with the "force of the universe" and the framework of the metaphysical laws that affect mankind is the path to maximize our existence, contributions, and consciousness.

Learning to use the mind and concentrate on our desires is where self actualization begins. Even the great Marconi was referred to the insane-asylum by government officials for suggesting that information and thoughts can be sent over the airwaves. However, today all of us know that we can tune into any given channel and send messages millions of miles. Harnessing the power of prayer, meditation and contemplation is where inspiration and well-being is cultivated. With this power of mental focus and cooperation with the universal law, we become masters of our destiny.

From Taoism to Christianity, and from Eastern and Western cultures, the mystics believed in a timeless and formless force that governs the cosmos. Most of the founding fathers of the United States were deists who believed in the Source or a supreme God. We are born of this cosmic force, and we have the ability to more effectively cooperate as spiritual and physical beings in conjunction with this force. Listen to your heart and allow yourself to become and evolve into your highest expression; get in tune with the world and allow yourself to manifest your Destiny and Bliss....

What Every Spiritual Seeker Should Know

Regardless of your culture and tradition, personal growth and expressing your best life should be your goal. If any researcher analyzes world history, the fundamental keys to peace and prosperity are rooted in MOST of the ancient mystery schools and the teachings within secret esoteric orders of the world. As you may assume, the question of a higher order, A Supreme Life Force, Philosophical Strategies, Creation Beliefs and the customs of the world have many common denominators. From the first Babylonian cuneiform text, to the teachings Oriental or Central-American Shamans, this manuscript shows and enlightens the reader about the history and evolution of spirituality and metaphysics.

As communities did thousands of years ago, people gather today to invoke the power of the universe and seek to communicate or harmonize with the Supreme. One only needs to watch the Matrix or Star Trek to imagine boundless universal powers of abundant possibility. However you may perceive the "powers of creation" and the "human mind", there has been much speculation on the ability of human and spiritual potential from the times of Socrates to the present day. A researcher does not need to work very hard to find that: spiritual masters, world leaders, religious gurus, and even present day CEOs have incorporated metaphysical exercises and practice in their daily lives to optimize their inner peace & outer success. As such, successful individuals are basically silent about what they personally engage to expand their spiritual mindset and achieve maximum performance and tranquility. It is generally accepted that leaders and successful people do not reveal or evangelize their beliefs and methods. In sum, there are various chapters and teachings in this book that address metaphysical practices. Leading American Judeo & Christian congregations, catechisms, and practices from the USA are intentionally <u>not</u>

<u>included</u> in this presentation due to lack of space. The objective of this book is to bring to light "the secrets" that American's don't normally learn about in their spiritual training. Also, probability - based spirituality or teachings included in astrology, I-Ching, Kabala, or Runes are also left out of this book due to the general complexity of these teachings.   After evaluating over 1000 authors in the area of metaphysics and experiencing various secret societies, spiritual groups, and organizations to further learn the best practices for holistic spiritual living, this manuscript was complied

Consciousness

What is consciousness? Many refer to the subconscious and the conscious mind as separated into two things. And the consciousness at it's foundation is composed of the 5 senses of: taste, feel, smell, and sound and vision. Those are the main five senses, and consciousness is generally operative on the levels of mind and memory. So, we are either working with what's going on in the present or you are drawing from your memory or a combination of both. And then there is how to train and use the consciousness with general practices and skills of the day. There is consciousness beyond the traditional senses which can be developed. Just think about what you may be conscious of on a daily basis such as your dreams, intuition, memory, mindfulness, prayer, daydreaming states, meditation, gut feelings, clairaudience, awareness, your sensations and various emotions of wisdom, awe, courage, love.   Two of the higher levels of consciousness and human development are: imagination and intuition. These two are available to all, but few know how to maximize these two aspects of self development, mind control, and consciousness. And the next level of consciousness which I refer to as C2K involves the use of imagination coupled with intuition, and developing those two parts of the mind to act with the power of synthesis of the totality of information. Other areas of training and development of consciousness are symbolism, metaphors, allegories, and parables. These tools and practices help us remember things, or act on information, and learn lessons, of course because we can play the tape back in our heads and respond to our perceptions according to our knowledge.

The Operative Areas of Philosophy and Consciousness

It seems that the entire essence of philosophical empowerment is to learn mastery over the dominant thoughts of your mind to produce greater rewards in your life in all three areas of: body, mind and spirit.

Mind is said to generally include various aspects of self or soul. You also have your consciousness or your sub consciousness. Further, even some form of super-consciousness may be available to us all in the form of inspiration and ideas coming to us at any given moment. In general, the ancient philosophers of our times have focused on many issues, but there's really three or four key areas of philosophical discussion that are primary for seeking peak potential.

Some of the greatest philosophers will say that each of us has untapped abilities or untapped talents that are seeking to express themselves from within us. Some of the great sages such as Emerson said that most people's problems result from authenticity and purpose being frustrated, which means the frustration of their potential talents. People want to be moving towards their life's purpose which should include a labor of love.

The famous philosopher Schopenhauer has formulated that the life force in all of us is demanding expression. That means we all have a willful purpose, like a flower which is meant to become a full flower, and a stallion is meant to become a stallion. Some of these philosophers say we must learn to use our willingness and master our willpower to express ourselves and our true essence.

And whether it's Hegel, Buddha, Einstein, or Marcus Aurelius, most of the greatest teachers will say that there is a spirit of the universe that allows us to function while using very impersonal laws. If we learn to cooperate with the impersonal laws, like gravity for instance, and higher laws than that, that we can talk about later, then we can master our destiny.

Some of the greatest writers such as Emmanuel Kant believed that happiness is a legitimate and noble goal for human beings, and that we should do that which makes us worthy of happiness. And to do that which makes us worthy of happiness, we have to master ourselves from the inside out, and that is what is called an inner or esoteric mastery. This is the most important type of justice which I call, ISJ Inner Social Justice.

And famous teachers such as Nietzsche have said that we have to master our will to express our true talents to the best of our ability. As for results, the famous psychologist and philosopher William James claimed that we need to just do what works, and that's part of pragmatism. Pragmatism says do the things that work, and avoid the things that don't work, and that also coincides with the famous emperor, Marcus Aurelius who advocated avoiding of ignorance while trying and do things that result in goodness, happiness, and integrity.

With all of that being said, Ralph Waldo Emerson has stated with great authority that, "Fortune is the fruit of character", and as we'll discuss later in this book, CHARACTER is a totality and a combination of our actions, our omissions, and the quality of our thinking, so a lot of this book is focused on mastering "who we are" the best of our ability. The famous theologian Thomas Aquinas wrote in "On the Heavens" that, "The study of philosophy has its purpose to know not what people have thought, but rather the truth about the way things are."

Furthermore, the famous philosopher Hegel said that objective analysis is an illusion, because things only exist in the context of the observer's perception of them. "Consciousness is as much part of the science as the world of objects that it purports to analyze." Therefore, Hegel's real blockbuster idea is that science is not the discovery of the world, but rather the comprehension of your own deeper mind or consciousness itself. This concept also relates to quantum physics in that the observer always affects reality at some level.

1) The Matrix or Framework Philosophy

The first philosophical concept to observe is the all-permeating framework of the universe and mankind. In theory, we must all submit to the principle that there exists an impersonal framework of universal laws which are applied to everyone equally. All of us have a mind, a body, and abilities to use on this planet to survive, grow, and interact with nature.

Civilization has evolved over thousands of years into a societal framework in which people give up certain freedoms so that they can be protected by a government or a sovereign nation. It's a give and take situation. So, we give up a bit of our freedom so that we can have the protections of government and the protections of law for life, liberty, and the pursuit of happiness for instance. We also want the governmental protection of our family, the right to possession of property, rights to hold beliefs, and the ability to engage business and keep profit. So, the first area of philosophy concerns our external environment.

2) Reality and the Senses – Perception Philosophy

The second area of philosophy that the gurus of the past discuss is how we perceive reality, or what is reality? And many of the philosophers will discuss the five senses of: taste, feeling, smell, sound, and sight/seeing. We utilize our ability of our five senses to perceive and gather reality, and then we might be able to harness a sixth sense which is something beyond our normal senses, which is our ability to have constructive: inspiration, intuition, impressions, and prescience.

How we perceive our reality is how we obtain and build the beliefs and the ideas and the preconceptions of our world. So, from the moment of birth up until today, we've gathered all of this information and accumulated these lessons, beliefs, ideas and conceptions. Moreover, we use these collected ideas to create a reality of the past and the present. We use our hopes and beliefs to color actually what we see, or to color our worldview as we perceive it moment by moment. So, this is the second major area of philosophy and metaphysics.

3) Innovation Philosophy – Changing Mind and Environment

And then the third area in philosophy that seems most innovative is how do we alter and change our beliefs and our consciousness. How do we modify our worldview and how we think for a better life? How do we change our destiny for the better?

On a basic level, if you're at an elementary school or very young, the teachers are going to train you to do certain things. Whether it's reading, writing, or arithmetic, or some type of physical education, they're actually teaching you and training your mind in how to work with language and other educational skills such as computers. Teaching children to communicate and interact. So, that's how you initially work with young people until they become adults and, of course, by that time they've accumulated vast experiences and beliefs into their consciousness and sub consciousness.

But the question for experts today is do we have the ability to shape our destiny and our future by manipulating our conscience and consciousness. If so, how much control can we have? Can we do that using certain tools or certain techniques or certain strategies for affecting our mind or mindset?

And that brings us really into where we are here with this book. In this book is included the great teachings of the past and present. We also have included the ideas of the great teachers from the East and the West, what have they had to say about the development of your mind. What have the great gurus said about creating an efficient and effective mindset that works in conjunction with your body, your mind, the universe or your environment? So, that is what this book is really going to focus upon. What have the great teachers said in creating and formulating a body of knowledge or constructive methods that anyone can use to transform their life. What techniques and ideas have the masters created to help regular folks change or enhance the direction of their life towards their dreams and towards their true authentic destiny.

Overall, the theme of this codex is teaching people how to obtain that one percent improvement in your life to put you above all others. To raise you from drowning to being above the water forever. Thoreau once specified that the objective is to go to a higher order of living by working with the impersonal laws of the universe.

This higher order of living isn't necessarily a 20% improvement or reaching 100%. It's actually a HUGE WIN if you can just improve daily life by one percent. Then, you will can change your life dramatically for the better. If you can operate at that one percent greater ability than other people, or other places and things, you will have an edge, a constant edge for the rest of your life with your body, mind, and your spirit.

In the end, as Dr. Pavlov stated, certain stimuli create certain responses. As with Pavlov, we need to appropriate the necessary mental and physical and spiritual stimuli, to stimulate the growth and success that we seek.

As such, if you begin to cooperate with: your mental abilities, the universe, and your God, then you will master the ability, using this harmonic existence, to maintain your body, mind, and soul at a more efficient and effective level. And it only takes a little bit of extra willingness, extra effort, extra persistence, and knowingness and belief to go beyond what other great people have done with their lives.

Magic: A Summary of Forgiveness, Awareness, and Unity

The philosophy of metaphysics contains many insights, ideas, and paths to obtain peace, love and forgiveness. One of the fundamental messages of the Course is the difference between reality and illusion and what is true about the way we think and what is false. For personal mastery, we must be able to identify what is part of our ego and what is part of our authentic self, or our spiritual self. The key to this first teaching is that nothing can really hurt what is inside of you, the real authentic you, your real spiritual self. Nothing can hurt that. No matter what happens to your physical body, there is a part of you that can never be hurt, which is part of the "Spirit of the Universe" and part of God. To really come into a knowing-ness of this teaching, you must believe that you are connected to the source of creation and that you are a child of creation. Once you can deeply feel that connection between your spirit and the universe, then you are linked with that connection where you can finally reach your authentic power and your potential.

Now we realize that it may be difficult for many of you to believe in a power greater than yourself or a God of your understanding can be a challenge for some people, however, it must be said that if you can embrace the principles or the path, or you can embrace the spiritual philosophy and the love of the universe. The key, honestly, is acknowledging that you are not god, and you are not in total control. I understand that can be a hard thing to swallow for some, but when you let go and allow the universe to be your guide and to cooperate with The G-FORCE, you receive POWER. That means you are deliberately and intently and mutually operating with and in the universe. You find it is easier not playing god, and you understand that the universe is the greater force that you can cultivate for your advantage. As soon as you begin to cooperate with that force and that concept, then you can become harmonious with the creative power. To cultivate flow or be in tune with the spirit and unified with it, that is the Quantum Leap to obtain enthusiasm and empowerment. The second step is about reality and trying to attack it or protect yourself or separate from it. The ego is constantly talking to you, trying to protect your ego-self from other people, to make yourself feel better about yourself or sometimes it's trying to make you feel worse about yourself. The secret is to transcend that false ego and let go of that ego mind and self talk that is not real, it's just ego-chatter-based opinions. By letting go and learning to filter, you can connect with that spiritual self and your mind will no longer be a "house divided."

That real self is authentic and that real self knows that you ARE a good and whole and complete perfect being. Unfortunately for many of us, the ego is driven by pride, lust, anger, greed, gluttony, envy and sloth. Ego is even driven by subtle discouragement or justifiable resentment. So this false-mind and ego needs this ego-food to empower itself and the key for us to live happily and efficiently and effectively is to quit feeding the ego with this type of negative nutrition that it loves.

This separation between us as spiritual children from "A God of our understanding" is a fallacy in the clouded mind. The key to spiritual power is to clear away the wreckage of the past, to clear away the mental garbage, to dissipate the pride and the anger and the greed and the discouragement and the resentment, to let all of that go, push it aside, work through it, talk to other people about it, pray about it. Pray for those in our past, to let go of them. Do these things to receive this gift of cleansing and catharsis so we can reconnect to our Christ selves or our holy spirit.

Thus, the Metaphysical Strategy IS the connection SECRET. Getting away from the separation and reconnecting to spiritual power is available for everyone who earnestly and sincerely wants it because it's always there. The miracle of unity is always available, the gift is always ready for those who are willing to accept it, but all of us must open our hearts and open our closed fists to receive this celestial reward.

Many hold on to old ideas and grievances. Many of us believe that we have sinned or that we have been bad people in the past, that we've done unforgivable harms. The real question of the day is will your God forgive you? Can you forgive yourself? And the answer is yes to both, if you are willing to allow yourself to be forgiven, if you are willing to forgive others and if you are willing to forgive God and if you are willing to allow God to forgive you. Then this forgiveness, this peace of mind, this peace that passeth all understanding can be available to you. It may take a little work but you can work through it. If you need help, you can always find a licensed counselor, a life coach, a priest, rabbi or an imam or even someone in a 12 step program. You can discuss privately these topics one-on-one and through private discourse. Also, you may discuss other important issues with your god of your personal understanding so that you may gain this peace and let go of these alleged sins.   The objective is to put past ideas which may be draining your energy in the past because you need this purity of mind, this clarity of mind so you can stay connected and operate at a higher order of being.

There comes a point where all of us have an ego-voice that wants to blame others or use resentments to justify ourselves or justify the way we feel about other people. We were trying to blame people, places and things for the way we feel about ourselves, or we're trying to blame people and institutions for our failures. Or, we're trying to use our resentments, blame or anger to justify our guilt or to understand our shame. But there comes a point where each and every one of us needs to let go of our shame. There comes a point where all of us have to say, "Nobody can shame me anymore, nobody can shame the authentic spiritual self that you have inside you."

In many religions, there comes a point where you become reborn, reinvented, reconnected or even re-baptized as an adult and your faith becomes alive again. With faith and earnest beliefs, you transcend hope and knowingness. You can achieve this higher level of real belief and faith. Ultimately, if you can cultivate and develop faith, that is where real happiness and real peace of mind comes from, because you've altered your thought patterns to a higher dimension.

In spiritual programs, you might hear someone talk about a spiritual awakening, becoming awake spiritually or even developing a sixth sense or higher consciousness. In some of philosophies where people may NOT believe or recognize a god, there are countless seekers who have cultivated faith and belief in conjunction with a power greater than themselves which could be the principles, path, or other set of devout values. To continue to grow spiritually, we need to work on what's called inner social justice or inner spiritual growth. Thus, if you are part of a spiritual program, it is contingent upon every one of us to build ourselves from the inside out using what is called "Inner Justice". Working on forgiveness, love, meditation, and love, we can continue to be in tune with the universe and solve our inner conflicts. This spiritual exercise allows us to maintain a harmonious relationship with ourselves, with God, with other people while improving self love, self regard, and love for the universe.

This is an extremely important magical and alchemical process, so let me say it one more time. The most important relationships you can cultivate is the one with yourself and your relationship with the force of the universe. By improving these mental concepts, you retrain your brain, create new empowering neuro-pathways, and the way you perceive yourself and your environment will dramatically improve.

The Holy Spirit or "God Force Energy"

What is that to us? Many people who have been reborn or reinvented in their faith because they have felt the spark of the inner Christ within them which may be called a reconnection. To put it into a simple allegory, let's pretend that there is a small fuse within your mind and that fuse can be blocked with emotions such as: anger and resentment or pride or jealousy or greed. All of these ills, what we would call deadly sins, affect the function of this "inner fuse of light".

Once you can clear out some of these blockages, like resentment, jealousy, anger or discouragement, the fuse lights up. And, that burning light is your connection between your spiritual self and the inner Christ which connects you to the source of all there is. This energy, enthusiasm, and the aliveness is the Holy Spirit, and that is what you hear people talk about who have been awakened.

It's a third force. It's you, the universe and something in-between that is a bright, magical connection and you know it when you have it. This inner awakening process does take persistence, but if you ask the universe to be connected to it, the power will materialize. If you ask for the release from bondage from self and from ego and ask for release from resentments and anger, blame, guilt and shame, then, you will know freedom. By doing all of these other things and allowing yourself to be set free, the inner-burning, bright, shining connection can be yours.

Some people might call this bright light a "spiritual awakening" or some people might refer to this in A Course of Miracles as the "holy instant", a moment where your connection is realized and you know you are cooperating or participating with a power greater than yourself fueled by love and where the ego is not controlling you. Then we can heal our perception by individually forgiving the world. We can change our hearts and minds when we decide earnestly to expand the way we think by asking ask the universe for help and by praying to receive this gift of a superior perception. Then, we can become awakened and alive and aware for truly the first time.

Changing our minds about the world and allowing the Holy Spirit to heal the way we feel, to heal our worldview, to heal the way we think is ultimately the key to freedom. And, once you embrace this Holy Spirit or this spiritual awakening, then you will have this expanded perception.

But first, you need to remember that you must clear away the mental debris of the past create fresh, empty space within your heart and within your mind – for new LIFE , for new and good and wholesome beliefs. Once you have cleared away the old ideas and made room for some good, then the spirit of the universe lights up within you, this inner Christ and this inner connection to the Holy Spirit and the universe becomes alive. You, in turn, become energized and then the way you view the world at any given moment becomes clear and augmented. If you have a consciousness of wealth or a consciousness of happiness or a consciousness of peace, at any given moment, it will then color the way you perceive that moment and the way you give purpose and meaning to your life.

There are many ways to heal our perceptions, but one of the best methods is to renew the mind, forgive yourself, to forgive other people and to forgive God. We do this because, let's face it, there are two relationships that are most important in your life – the relationship with yourself and the relationship with a power greater than yourself which most simply call GOD. These two relationships can make or break you. Those two relationships can make life easy or make life a struggle and as many spiritual programs profess, struggle is not necessary. Needless struggle is not mandatory. A lot of people, a lot of us, want to hold onto these old ways, hold onto these old habits, this old way of thinking because it gives us adrenaline and it makes us feel better than other people. It allows us to forget about our failures when, in fact, if we could let go of negative thinking and let go of these destructive habits, then our authentic selves can blossom and we can become who we really are meant to be. Further, we can become connected and have this intuition and this creativity that we're really supposed to utilize that makes us feel alive, that makes us feel authentic, and that makes us feel like we have purpose. Finally, we will then feel that we are truly heading down the path that we were always meant travel.

If you are having trouble with forgiveness, then we can offer several different methods to fix that problem or to cure that problem. The first one is every day when you wake up and every night before you go to bed, start saying affirmations aloud or to yourself or even in the mirror. You can write your own affirmations or you can go to the store and buy a book on affirmations and prayers to read silently or aloud. Many read these prayers or these meditations to themselves, or even read them out loud or to another person who loves and supports you. Some may read them in conjunction with working with a spiritual counselor, sponsor, or a life coach. Read affirmative literature each day in the morning and in the evening and your beliefs and your worldview will change. Your vibration and energy will be altered upward. Your mindset will be enhanced and you will obtain a sense of excellence and poise. Sometimes it takes 30 days before you even feel a major change or a major effect, but it will come quickly and powerfully. You may not even notice it but I promise you that if you do these practical-magical exercises for 30 days where you focus on gratitude, on peace of mind, & on forgiveness, you will become spiritually free and empowered.

If you have problems even beyond that, challenges even that you think are too heavy for basic prayers and affirmations, I recommend that you hit your knees every morning and every night and you ask directly to the God of your understanding for help. Or, you simply ask the Holy Spirit or Jesus Christ or ask your favorite Saint for intercession or assistance. It doesn't need to be perfect, as you simply need to humble yourself and tune in to the SOURCE and ask if you can be assisted and offer to cooperate. That's it. You will be amazed with the power you receive. The key is that you earnestly make petition direct to God and say, "Please forgive me, please heal me, please remove my resentments, and please take away my dislike or my hatred for this person or for myself."

Or you may even pray for the happiness of another person or other individual, you pray earnestly and ask God to bless them and to take them away from your thinking. Ask your higher power to bless everyone, to bless those in your family, in your household, but most importantly, ask for grace for yourself, ask for peace for yourself, and ask for a thankful heart for yourself. Become a person who praises other people or even blesses your very self. Become a person who speaks of constructive and grateful and thankful things and if you do all of this, you will have what is called a grateful heart. You will have a firm belief and faith in the universe because it will change your faith in mankind. Many of us have had some really tough challenges. An example might be the death of someone close in your family or a family member or a great sickness or a catastrophic event such as a hurricane or a tsunami, whatever it might be. Some of us may have experienced a business divorce, a family divorce, your parents divorcing, or even yourself. All of these things can be extremely challenging and when we get into these situations that are extremely challenging, it's a call for many of us to rise to the occasion and become stronger.

Many times, we are going to have to release the other people that are involved whether it's a business problem with a partner or a lawsuit or a divorce or even a situation with our children. We're going to have to release people, release them with love, pray for them, pray that we can forgive them, and pray that they can forgive us. If we are able to do these things and to let go of what's hurting us and to become free and awake and aware while in forgiveness, all of these things provide us a true perception. This authentic perception looks past the bodily illusion to the light of Christ, and we will begin to see the little bit of God that is in all people. When we finally reach this spiritual awake-ness and clarity, then the Holy Spirit will lift us up and make us whole. However, there is an investment that we have to make in maintaining this spiritual condition and a lot of it comes by using a basic methodology and some fundamental tools herein. So to maintain our spiritual condition, we're probably going to need to do spiritual things and act responsibly. What we mean by that is to respond in a spiritual way to life and if that becomes difficult, of course, then you will have to continue to work the steps hitherto and continue to integrate the healthy virtues and ethics of the philosophy of your understanding or archetype.

We practice these spiritual exercises to maintain clarity, to maintain forgiveness, to maintain some sense of purity of mind.

Purity of mind is where you are acting with love and unselfishness and you have a mindset of clear-and-convincing gratitude. That's what we mean by purity of mind and if you're doing things on a daily basis to maintain this quality of mind and quality of spirit and quality of perception, then that inner Christ, that inner light will remain bright and protect you because you will be acting in concert and in cooperation with the pure force of creation. Similarly, many of us will need to deeply consider how we can continue to look at our character development. We enhance our character by observing the way we're acting, not acting, and the ways we're thinking. Maybe at the end of the day, take some notes about how you acted and think about ways that you can become a better person. Even 200+ years ago, Benjamin Franklin, in his autobiography, talked about his devotion to this evening practice of taking an inventory of his day with the motive of trying to become a better person tomorrow. By prayer and meditation and maintaining this sufficient humility of which we've talked about, we will maintain some sense of clarity and spirituality in our lives. What we mean by humility are 4 key attributes: that you understand that you are teachable; that you understand your true authentic place in this world; that you are connected to a power greater than yourself; and that you understand who you really are. Humility is really the opposite of the insane ego-driven grandiosity or self-defeating thinking that inhibits our happiness. These practices are designed to eliminate the blocks to your connection to the spirit. If we desire to maintain our spiritual condition, then what will be important is our dedication to prayer, meditation, humility, clarity, love, and forgiveness. By virtue of our efforts, we become operative at a higher order and this higher state blesses us with a unity to a power greater than ourselves. Then, we finally understand our true identity and our sonship with God.

12 Steps to Prosperity - Summary of Teachings

Here are 12 Steps to Extreme Wealth & Prosperity with Descriptions

Read these 12 steps. Take notes. Try and understand how these steps work together. The rest of the book is packed with ideas of success, summaries of 25 great self help writers and strategies for wealth, health and happiness.

1. **Beliefs, Clearing, and Programming** - Develop a strident belief that the Universe wants the best for you at all times and will provide for you at all times if you cooperate with the immutable laws of achievement. **Purify – Learn to Diagnose Problems, Identify Opportunities, Empty Problems and Fill with Desire, Objectives, and Potential.** Become ready and willing to write your own horoscope and program your own mind with the destiny you seek. Release and repudiate petty external forces that affect your dominant thought patterns and ability to reach your potential. **Decide What is True?** Determine what ideas to accept as true. Use the ideas that work best to be a pragmatist. If you are lacking in health and prosperity, you may have a subconscious mindset of unworthiness, shame, scarcity and frustration or feelings of anger. **Rewrite Your Drive** - These old ideas can be overwritten, they can be dissipated with effort, using emptying and filling strategies. **Reject Bullshit** - You must deny and reject what you don't what in your life and purge old non-constructive ideas.

2. **Renew Mind** – Refining and Defining the MINDSET into the consciousness that You Seek. Do what you need to do to purge the ideas and thoughts that do not serve your happiness and success. Clear your mindset for a new and improved set of beliefs and objectives. When your mental and spiritual hard drive is clear, it becomes ready for a new set of programs and performance. **Choice** - Our greatest power is the power of choice and action. We can be discerning in what we bring into our mind, lives, and hearts. There is power in bold thinking and actions. **Writing goals** down helps you impress the objectives on your mind and stay a few chess moves ahead which opens up opportunities and ideas. . Always write out what you want, putting pen to paper clarifies and distills your focus and purpose. Write out the **incremental steps** to achieve your goals. If you type them, put them where you can see them every day. Nobody knows you better than yourself. If you can tune into your higher self, you can illuminate and discover your authentic purpose and desires. **Flow of Ideas** - If you can get into a meditative place and relax, you can allow the inspiration of the universe or the ideas of the universe to come to you. You can act on this higher will by analyzing those ideas. If the ideas are honest, mindful, unselfish, and loving, you will find great power in these ideas.

3. **Declare Your Aims** – Choosing what you want to be, do, and have. At some point, we must pick what we will do with our time and abilities and focus our desires on what we want to do and where we want to go. Think beyond what you have been told you can do or achieve**, question YOURSELF**. What else am I missing or truly seeking to be, do, or have? **Affirmations** help re-write your neuron connections and DNA. Leaving new imprints on your mind of the reasonableness of success is

important. Learning to believe that success and happiness is a reasonable option can transform your life's direction for the better. Try mental affirmation, visual, verbal auto suggestion, notes, signs, symbols, charms, poetry, music, video, trance, and dance. **Visualize** what you want to be, do. and have. Release the mental masterpiece of your "completed goals" into the world and allow the universe to work on it for you at night while you sleep. **Augment the Senses** - The next day, practice imagining the life you aspire to achieve. To learn to see and feel your desired destiny while picturing yourself utilizing the excellent results in your deeper mind with emotion and sensation.

4. **Charge Your Brain** – Charging your purpose and belief with intent and emotions such as love and aliveness. When we take command of our thoughts and emotions, we can take control of the direction of our life. **Hacking Fortune and Fate** – In ancient Europe, there are myths about fate which are referring to the three maidens of fortune. In Rome they called them the Fortuna, in Scandinavia, they were called the Three Norns or Fates. They were said to weave the future. There is the maiden of the past, the maiden of the present, and maiden of the future or "what will be". It is important to weave your own destiny by contributing energy and mindful acts to the NOW to create a pattern of the past which combined with actions and thinking of today, manifests the future of possibilities.

Thankfulness - After researching human performance for decades, it is also critical to integrate a worldview of opportunity and possibility. This can be done by incorporating gratitude and thankfulness into your daily life. Gratitude is an ingredient of "peace of mind" and love. Such a powerful ingredient can allow your mind and brain to function at a higher level of clarity. Rather than incessantly focusing on what is wrong, if we can refocus on what is good and right with our home, relationships, and life; then, we can cultivate a mindset of contentment, prosperity and abundance. Gratitude has a special power to keep us in harmonious relationship with the spirit and laws of the universe. It is important to purge your mind, through a process letting go of the dead weight of: resentments, anger, unworthiness, or even hatred. With this clearing work, we can then learn to fill our minds with powerful and constructive thoughts of courage, patience, kindness, love, peace, humility, love, and generosity. Accordingly, the best way to charge the brain with productive dominant thoughts is to dedicate your thinking toward a dominant mindset of positivity and harmony.

5. **Empower Yourself** – Respect yourself and your inner esoteric power. Learning to understand and respect the immutable laws of the universe, will allow you to work in harmony with the elements. **Harmoniousness** - Master harmony with self and with others. A harmonious mindset attracts and deserves wealth and health because it is open to good and vibrates in a way that does not repel abundance. Remember that if you are always vibrating mentally about such ideas as: negative thoughts, jealousy, envy, or resentments; then, your inherent state of being may actually repel your opportunities or good people. However, if your mindset is one of enthusiasm, worthiness, aspiration, harmony and success, then you would be mentally more aware of opportunities and have a clear ability to respond. **Worthiness** – You must decide, internalize, and act as if you are worthy of life's blessings. What is your

self image consciousness and dominant self image thought? You only receive what you subconsciously allow yourself to have. The better you treat yourself; the better quality of people you will have in your life. **Mental Relationships** Cultivate a harmonious positive relationship with health, self, love and wealth. Master body, mind, and spirit through exercise you enjoy, a healthy diet, periodic fellowship, and healthy REM sleep. With this balance you can also boost your mind by learning new skills and tactically enhancing your performance toward your goals. Become connected with the powers of the universe rather than disconnected.

6. **Purpose & Viewpoint** – A mindful worldview changes experience and experience changes consciousness. Being mindful and introspective while in action is the key to efficiency and effectiveness. **Unambiguousness** - Be definite about what you want and know how to ask for it. Know how to illuminate your "elevator pitch" of goals to your mind and God. **Articulate Mental Energy into The Universe** - You may need to affirm and decree "in prayer and aloud" the things that you want so as to best imprint the objectives into your deeper mind. Model yourself after the tactics of great leaders and winners but find your own style and authenticity. It is said that one of the only ways to increase efficiency of a worker already using proven strategies of success is to allow them to have and master their own style. **Be Authentic** - **"You See, You Be, You Are"** - **UC=UB=UR** – What you dominantly see yourself as being in your mind is what you become and what you become is what and who you ARE ….

7. **Love** – Be in love with your soul and with your inner spirituality. Self love is extremely powerful and manifests as

charisma and enthusiasm. Controlling your charisma can make you into a powerful relationship builder whether in business, private life, or business negotiations. **Radiate Zeal** - Love your inner higher self, love what you desire, love what you seek and what you need.   When you love yourself, you will love others. When you allow yourself to love others, you will love yourself better.   **Connectedness** - Your harmonious connection to the universe is the foundation of your power and awareness. Possessing clarity of mind is like having a computer that is not overloaded with junk and is virus free. Remember, most people believe that the spark of creation is within themselves. Learn to love and value that spark that connects you to the vast energy of creation.

8. **Decree** – Speak of what you want in your mind and out loud. A decree can be verbal, mental, prayerful, mindful, written, or put down into the form of a sign, symbol, musical composition, poem, charm/sigil, video, or dance. Use these forms of incantations and written commands to program your mind and beliefs to achieve peak potential. Make sure happiness, love, success, and financial freedom matter to you. **Impress Your Mind** - How will you continue to impress the life you want and deserve upon your subconscious mind? You can use specific goal selection, tactical training, imagination, visualization, auto-suggestion, brain training, self talk, affirmations, notes to yourself, mapping, treasure maps, and more.

9. **Aliveness** - Live Well – Learn to plan, act, survive, excel, live, love, and enjoy. Learning what you love to do while learning to enjoy your success. Allow yourself the relationships, assets, and opportunities you deserve. **Prepare the table** – Prepare

for what you seek, keeping in mind that you must be able to receive your good. Prepare your mind, body, appearance, skills, etc. **Comprehension** - You must comprehend what you want (who, what when, and how) <u>of what you seek to be, do, or have.</u> You must learn to have the success in your mind's eye, have your mind know how to accomplish it, know and be the success before it happens, to accomplish your goals.

10.   **Acceptance** - Refuse to accept struggle. Demand improvement and incremental success in your life and your mindset. Break out to accept new greatness of your life. ACCEPT YOUR GOOD and LET GO of NEGATIVE THINKING. Be a champion and ditch the blaming and complaining. **Remain Tuned in to Opportunities** - Keep your conscious mind tuned in/aware of the good we desire and deserve. You want a good life with the freedom to work and travel, when and where you want. Maintain intense awareness of your acts, words, and deeds. **Maintain Receptiveness** - Make clear to your mind what you want. Speak to your mind and send images of success to it during receptive moments of the day. Keep your primary purpose at the forefront of your heart, mind, and subconscious.

11.   **Wisdom** – Every idea or goal may require you to obtain new knowledge. Find out what you need to know to accomplish your goals. Cultivate your mind, body and spirit in order to maximize your potential for yourself and those you love. **Find Joy** - Scan your memory for instances which gave you joy. What was in those moments? Was it travel, people, winning, achieving peace that you felt while using your skills? What energizes you? Find your labor of love, your calling, and you will serve humanity, enjoy wholeness, and achieve

success. Align with those who you are supposed to be in this period of your life. Alignment and wisdom work with each other to give you peace, power. and poise. Wisdom comes from the universe. Stay tuned into it, maintain clarity of mind, seek inspiration, and act on great ideas.

12.   **Action** – Why not start reaching your goals today? Go after it. Go and be it. Go and have it ! Take ownership of and responsibility for your destiny. Seize upon 2 or 3 things to do each day toward your optimum health, happiness, success, and relationships. Take a moment to praise yourself for something done well today. Praise somebody else for doing something with excellence. Take command of assets and money. Making assets and money serve you. Use your money wisely to invest in body, mind, and soul growth. Invest in your loved ones, and invest in your opportunities. **Self Motivation** is critical. We must manipulate our minds into continuous improvement of doing, acting, making phone calls, emailing, marketing, closing deals, working out, preparing, and performing. **Pragmatism** - Exceptional dedication, imagination, practice, and preparation equals exceptional results. **DO WHAT WORKS** - Don't worry about the WHY, please just do the things that result in success for those who have had success, or replicate the actions of the most happy or successful people you admire. If you don't know what works, ask them.

The best way to begin these steps is to take a hard look at your track record for the last 1-5 years. Were the last few years a good period in your life? Can you do better? Do you want more? As a law professor, I would say that you either have a good case or a bad one. You either have the law on your side or not. You either have quality evidence to support your claim or your don't. You can either win or lose.

In law, if you can win a case by a preponderance of the evidence which is just a level of proof that is greater than 50%. Life can be the same. If you are operating at a level of 49% or less, you are losing at the game of life each day. If you can improve by just more than 1+%, you are now considered a winner in the metaphysical court of laws. It is just that simple! Once you believe that you are happy, healthy and prosperous 51% or more of the time; then, you are above water and you may continuously feel like you have super human abilities in contract to before.

When discussing the greatest philosophers and psychologists, it is hard to miss their emphasis on human potential and human performance. Top thinkers of the past put a focus on character, thinking, habits, and skills, but they also focus on the use of the consciousness.   With the great Ralph Waldo Emerson, he suggested in his writings that fortune is the fruit of your character, and the great Descartes mused over how mankind is equipped to rule over nature and be creative in a way that expresses excellence. From the Stoics to Jeremy Bentham, great thinkers have stated that minimizing struggle is a key objective in maximizing pleasure and success.

If you are familiar with the Danish Philosopher Soren Kierkegaard, his writings illuminate that life can be viewed as a task based on the free, responsible choices of individuals which is an existentialist viewpoint. As individuals, Kierkegaard suggested that seekers should detach themselves from the herd mentality, and discover their own world view and nurture their own unique meaning for life. However, our world-view is subject to many key variables. If we learn to manipulate the variables and cooperate with the principles of nature, we can achieve a greater self actualization. Self actualization is the degree to which an individual's predispositions are expressed in talents and work. [i] The prime determinants of professional behavior are to be found in the need for love, esteem, and self expression and self-actualization. [ii]

According to Schopenhauer, the phenomenal world is not so chaotic but rather operates according to sufficient reason or a set of guidelines. Schopenhauer implies that the immutable laws of the universe operate with causality or "cause and effect.' Schopenhauer also sees willpower as a kind of force that is always seeking higher expression that strives to not only survive but to grow.

Dr. Victor Frankl, espoused that life always has meaning even if that meaning or purpose is not clear at the time. Frankl believed that each person comes into life with unique potentialities to fulfill.   To make it more personal, my father, Judge/Sgt. Henry Mentz, believed that his purpose or meaning for his platoon in 1945 was to win the war in Europe, liberate the people, and free the starving prison camp survivors such as Dr. Victor Frankl.

Dr. William James, the father of modern psychology believed that if we can minimize the gap between our potential and our self actualization, we will have a higher self-regard. Similarly, Carl Jung, who is the godfather of "Analytical Psychology" believed that Individuation is becoming what you always were meant to be [*potentia* (Latin)] where you fulfill your unique purpose. Dr. Jung famously said, "Spiritus contra spiritum" which literally translates to "spirit against spirit". Loosely translated, it refers to a spiritual experience as the most effective way to counter a deadly affliction of the spirit such as addiction. As with Spinoza, Einstein believed that the universe is governed by impersonal natural laws where Einstein actually said, "I believe in Spinoza's God". Einstein probably meant that there is substance in all things that may be unseen much like in quantum physics, but if you can grasp how to harmoniously cooperate with the immutable laws of your environment, you can and will prosper at a higher level than others but that does not mean perfection or the elimination of the glitches in the scatter chart of life's success probabilities.

There are various laws that we take for granted such as the laws of electricity, thermodynamics, aerodynamics, principle of least resistance, and so forth. For example, the path of least resistance is the physical or metaphorical pathway that provides the least resistance to forward motion by a given object or entity, among a set of alternative paths. With the use of the mind and action, there are various ways to cooperate & engage people places and things. Sometimes, it is best to avoid some people places and things altogether to maximize success. To engage in lifelong learning, to avoid dangerous situations, and to maximize strength in "body, mind and spirit" are all excellent ways to lead a more efficient and effective lifestyle. However, you can do many things right, but if you still do "one thing" incessantly destructive, you can ruin your life and progress regardless of your good and amiable traits. I have seen celebrities, rock stars, royalty, and millionaires lose everything to drugs and addictions while also going to the gym, doing yoga and attending church each week. So, the moral of the story is to maximize constructive behavior and stay clear of destructive things. Get a plan and use methods and activities to expand your life, love, and friendships.

If you can dig deep and change yourself from the inside out, and begin to use great habits on a daily basis, you begin to stack the cosmic cards of life in your favor and you win at life's celestial casino going forward. Famous sales gurus often say that the difference between failure and great success can be as little as 2% more effort each day than other folks. Thus, we must all learn to control our dominant thoughts and habits while rejecting and avoiding needless scarcity and struggle based thinking. All pessimists have is their opinion of failure and "they are determined to be right about what is wrong with this world." As they say, belief is the acceptance of something as truth. Once you accept a belief, that acceptance begins to create new realities for you and you begin to experience life in a whole new way.

In conclusion, there are no poor people but rather only those who are determined to struggle without advancement. Wealth can be defined as the state of being "rich in life" including possessing the material prosperity to meet your needs. Wealth is also considered to be: relative health, wholeness, personal success, and a general feeling of prosperity. Learn to rely more on your higher self, your inner consciousness, and your 6th sense. If you are working these steps, you will have more ideas, more creativity, and more persistence to go after what you seek to expand your life. Life, in general, will meet you in the way that you reach out and greet life and seek abundance. We may all reap benefits from what we sow, but reaping requires us to take action each day, plant the seeds of ideas, give our all, and manifest successful tasks and goals one-by-one. With our continued expansion and growth in the garden of life, our harvest will be great.

The 12 Characteristics of Magical and Prosperous People

1. **A purpose driven personality** with a desire to express themselves in the most constructive ways.
2. **A worldview and consciousness of possibility,** prosperity and harmlessness
3. People who are beyond competitive and very creative. Visionaries who strive to see and feel the reality of their dreams.
4. **Gratitude minded** – people with a thankful heart and sincere belief in the goodness of the universe.
5. **Boldness, action oriented**, willing to take calculated risks, and Authentic.
6. Self Regard – people who believe that they are worthy of a rich and full life and are willing to work to receive it.
7. **At-Ease – Harmonious mind and thinking**. People willing to cultivate peace of mind and balance in body, mind and spirit.
8. **Love of Fellowship** – willing to help others with time and talent.
9. **Receptivity** - Global & Non-judgmental openness to others' ideas and creativity. Open to inspiration.
10. **A Unique Spirit** – Individualization of soul and spirit. Allowing yourself to become who you are meant to be.
11. **Desire to serve humanity** be being your best. A passion to contribute as an individual to the greater good.
12. **Spiritual Awakenings** - People who have become Spiritually Awake to a higher order of being and work to maintain such a level of thinking, acting and being.

The Power of Consciousness in the Now - Presumption Decoded

Being Contemplative in Action – Getting Into NOW

If you have ever thought deeply about the magical power of the present moment, you may wonder if you have the capability of this type of superior focus and mindfulness. After reviewing all of the major religions on the philosophy on the power of PRESENCE, I have discovered many specific keys to success in being in the moment. To begin with, the theme of the Power of Awareness is to quiet the mind, to calm the self-talk, to learn to control your thoughts while directing your thinking so that you may be present in the moment, to be alive and conscious "right now".

This is not necessarily a Eastern or Western concept, however there are many esoteric & Christian underpinnings herein that are addressed. Firstly, it is advised that we intently listen to our self-talk deep within our mind and then try to truly see and listen to that inner-voice as an observer. Getting to know your ego voice as compared to your authentic spiritual voice of your heart is also a major exercise of this topic.

The easiest example of directing your awareness to the now is to direct your controlled attentiveness to your body, to your breathing, to what you see, what you hear, what you're eating or what you're tasting or who you're with. Whether it's focusing on the aliveness of your child or actually seeing or sensing parts of your own body, you can go deeper into your awareness. Here's an example: Try to actually feel your extremities, actually noticing the feelings in your fingers or feelings in your toes at any given moment. Or, what emotions are going on in your mind or even in your stomach.

If you're like the average person, your mind could be harping on 50 different things at once, like a TV on 50 different channels constantly running, and the real key is to pick a channel and focus on a single concept, one thing at a time, one moment at a time, one day at a time, one instance at a time. Further, we can concentrate on one thing at a time, or we can just be aware to the moment and allow our mind to do what is best for us.   As an example, the famous movie The Last Samurai with Tom Cruise, they were talking about no mind. To NOT overthink everything is what a teacher would mean by no mind, not overthinking every single move or every single tactic.   And just like driving, the first time you drive the car or stick shift, there's many things that you're learning how to do that sooner or later becomes something embedded in your subconscious or in your machinery, and you automatically can get in a car and know exactly what you need to do. So the key really is to be able to program the way you live to think and live in a way that doesn't require you to overthink everything. This process allows you to exist in your real-time state of aliveness.

After rereading books on mysticism and self empowerment, many of us have an awakening of consciousness, a spiritual awakening of sorts, and don't even know how it happened or what had happened and years later we figure out that as a byproduct of reading what other mystics had taught about these types of transformations, we become better people. However, there are many of us out here in the world who have already had this similar type of awakening, this aliveness, this consciousness, and if you are one of us, you know it deeply. If you're on an enlightened path, you will inherently know it because you can walk in a room with 100 people in it, and you can look around and you actually see people and you're actually alive and you actually know what is happening. And if you're living in this awake-ness, you will have the ability to control what's going on in your mind and your thoughts, and you will have the ability to choose and decide the type of thinking that you will have all day long, and in the end the type of thinking that you have all day long, the type of actions you do all day long, the person who you are, who you become all day long. Then that's who and what you REALLY are. That is what you will become. So in total, if you're able to control your thinking and you're able to control who you are and the totality of your actions and inactions; then, you're entirely able to control your destiny and you're able to control what you become.

In books such as the Power of Now, Teachers such as Eckhart Tolle spend a lot of time talking about "no mind" and pain body. And I'm just going to explain it to you right now. Pain body is basically Eckhart Tolle's way of saying that if you're one of these people that's sitting around each day thinking negative thoughts and destructive thoughts and trying to be the victim and trying to identify with all this negative stuff and complaining all the time while also trying to blame everyone except yourself or your situation, That is the pain body.   You can learn about ego related negativism in church, from a life coach, or in various spiritual venues. However, Tolle's book s was the most popular manuscript to codify the concepts.

And what I'm saying is that if you have this ego that's wrapped up in this identity and it's trying to protect itself, it's not going to want to take a look in the mirror. Your ego is not going to want to change. It's not going to want to accept responsibility for your life and the way you are and what's become of you. So if you can break free of that ego bondage and find your spiritual self, your true inner self, who you really are and get in touch with that and get in touch with the spirituality within, then all the sudden this unlimited flow and this unlimited potentiality becomes available to you, and that's where this aliveness comes from. And, that's what the Christians talk about being *contemplative in action* and also Christians also talk about the Holy Spirit, which is basically that connectedness and that non-separateness, that *spiritual, god-unity* that every religion around the world talks about.

Once you enter this aliveness and this newfound awakening and this consciousness, you'll have no need to defend yourself. You'll have no desire to overreact to things. You'll have this true power within. And also you'll have this now consciousness, which determines how you effectively manifest things. Let's put it this way: if you're able to develop a new consciousness of aliveness, a higher consciousness of success, a greater consciousness of action and doing things, this ***"in the moment"*** consciousness is what will transmute ideas into success and transform possibility into taking mental form, bring ideas into material tangible form on this plane.

In many other religions or spiritual movements, you'll hear the word 'acceptance' and being able to accept what is. It is what it is or accept the now or accept the good and accept the bad and let go of it. Because this is in essence what will free you from present pain in the mind that's saying that you should be in pain.

Furthermore, this idea of knowingness is what you really want. You want to know and believe that you could control your destiny, and if you don't know and you don't believe, then you might be sitting around wishing for something to happen or hoping for something to happen, and it can keep you stuck in the past, or the future. And it can keep you from realizing your dreams if your ego and your "self" is so identified with things that are wrong with the world. If you can change your train of thoughts and change how you think, you'll be able to have your mind focus on what is right with the world and look at what is good and what is beautiful. And if you start focusing on all the good and the beautiful and the rightness and the righteousness of the world and its impersonal nature, you'll be able to attract more of that.

The Power of Esoteric Spirituality and Metaphysics

In essence, developing metaphysical power is an inside job. This is an esoteric science, this power of now. So being able to control what goes on the inside is esoteric and it's what spiritual and religious and philosophical leaders have been talking about since Pythagoras, Socrates, Plato, Confucius, Buddha, Aristotle and all the rest. They've been talking about these metaphysical concepts since the beginning of civilization. If you can master yourself, you'll be able to master your destiny and have a great effect upon those around you and do a great service for humanity.

What is great about The Power of Now or being in the moment with your consciousness, it allows you to compartmentalize the day, which keeps you from being paralyzed by any situations and you're able to free the mind of attachments. And if you can free the mind of too much junk that's floating around in it, you're able to focus and concentrate and direct your energies into the areas that will most improve your life from the inside out.

Additionally, attention is energy, so you need to remember what you focus on expands in your life. You need to choose and decide what to energize with your attention in any given moment. So like I said before, the pain body is this negative energy of the ego mind, and if you're able to get your attention away from that and give your attention to things that are constructive and positive and reinvigorating, then that's what you want to do because if you give your attention to the pain body, guess what? That's fuel that will keep pain flowing and going. Those who teach about the power of the PRESENT also write a lot about how your conscious mind and your subconscious mind coexist, or rather, how to transcend your ego elf to begin to listen to your spiritual voice.

It's like this, all of us really need to tap into that spiritual self, which is basically the best friend that you had growing-up when you were child. Now you know that there's an old adage that says that some children have their little best friend, their *imaginary* friend, which is really their spiritual higher-self that they are embracing and befriending and their imagination allows them to love that part of themselves without limitation. However, a lot of children lose that magical relationship at a very early age.

We know this story. We've seen it time and time again, so we know that this spiritual self, this best friend, that's the relationship that we need to cultivate. The relationship with our spiritual self and our relationship with the spirit of the universe should come first for us to maximize our peace and prosperity.

So anyway, some of these famous authors of days gone by have said that when you have a grateful mind and a thankful heart, it is a lot easier to have a living faith. Thus a mind of joy cannot support pain body or negative thinking. So the best thing that we can all do for ourselves to change our worldview is to change how we think and change our state of gratitude. As the famous philosopher Magus Incognito once said, each person's worldview is based on their spiritual condition.

So the word 'alchemy' really is transmuting one substance into another substance, and here if you could change your lower self into your higher self, if you could transcend from your ego into your spiritual essence, that is the real key to these teachings. Transmutation is achieved by the conscious contact with the spirit of the universe. Transmutation is achieved through the consciousness of love, the consciousness of wisdom, the consciousness of gratitude and joy.

The other issue in the power of the moment is how many of us are addicted to the adrenaline of anger or self-righteousness or justified anger and blame, and unfortunately that's why social justice has become such a trendy thing is because it can get you so riled up about blaming somebody for something that happened a long time ago when in essence if we focused all that very same time and energy for inner social justice, the whole world would probably change for the better.

And the other thing of this is that if we surround ourselves with sick people, angry people, people who are not alive, people who are realists, who think the world is bad, that type of attitude is contagious, and unfortunately as spiritual seekers, we want to be close to those who want a spiritual life.

And if we can draw close to those who have the same general desire of wholeness and aliveness and health, then we will all become healthier much quicker, and this of course is why self-help groups and fellowships of sorts have become so popular over the last 30, 40, 50 years.

And really the theme of NOW reminds of flow, reminds me of detachment. Meister Eckhart talked a lot about detachment. And we're talking about non-resistance, and there's just so many times in our lives where you can just let go and thrive. Accordingly, some of the biggest miracles in our lives happen when we're not fighting something, we have our mouths shut and we just allow things to pass us by. We have to know when to FLOW and when to pick our battles and know when to stand up for ourselves, but in general,

99% of the time we're going to be okay if we can just stay calm in the moment and allow people to just be.

Once you have developed this aliveness and this consciousness, this higher order in your life, you know what it tastes like and you're going to want more of it, and you're going to do the things that you can do to stay in tune and embrace and own it because it feels so good to be alive and to be clear and if we keep our minds somewhat clear and we do the things we need to do each day or each week to maintain like to spirit, that clarity and that peace of mind will be available and afforded to us.

In the end, this is about surrender. It's about "surrender to win". If you let go of the things that are hurting you, you're able to move forward and not have to drag a lot of dead weight along with you anymore. And then you'll learn to act with purpose and clarity and focus because you're not carrying all this useless baggage. And, then you'll learn to do all you can in the now. And this surrender really unveils your spiritual power.

So in essence, a lot of religions and movements, spiritual groups talk about this key to power, being free and clearing the mind. When you're able to master yourself, you're able to let go of all the junk in the past, you're able to create this space inside of you and allow some joy and greatness to come into your life for the first time.

Some people refer to it as a spiritual vacuum, and this vacuum, once you clear stuff out, it creates space in a vacuum and something has to fill it. And if you're in the power of now and you have this consciousness of good and you believe and you know that the world will take care of you in spite of everything that's going on, then good things will come to you. Good people, good ideas, good opportunities, good health and so forth will all be available to you.

So in summary, what is The Power of Now to me and what can it be to you? It's developing this relaxed and free awareness of the now, of the moment and in that relaxed free awareness you become receptive and awake to the good and the beautiful things in the world such as gratitude, health, aliveness, optimism, knowingness, and you're "I am-ness" or "spiritual and divine energy/presence" is made available to you. And what is the "I am"? The "I am" is your presence, is your spiritual self that is talked about in the old wisdom literature. And you become conscious of the now field of energy, which you will master and learn to control what is in that energy, that totality of it, and that becomes who you are.

And if you're anything like me or other people, when you wake up one morning, after having been engaging gratitude in your daily life and you begun clearing the baggage out of your past and using these methods and these steps of developing clarity, you begin letting go of all of the mental rubbish or clutter that has weighed you down. Then, you will find that you want to practice gratitude on a daily basis, you start to practice peace of mind on a daily basis and cultivating a thankful heart and a thankful mind on a daily basis. And behold, one morning sometime soon you're going to REALLY wake up and you're going to wake up on the RIGHT side of the bed, and you're going to KNOW it. And then a few days later, if you keep practicing this consciousness of love and consciousness of God and consciousness of good, you might wake up again like that, and then all of the sudden you'll continue to wake up on the right side of the bed and you'll look forward to the days and you'll be alive and want to do things each day for yourself and other people and participate in life.

And all of that aliveness and that now-ness and that spiritual awakeness is what dissipates this pain body and this negative thinking.

So in conclusion, you and a lot of other people, once you become awake, you're going to be so thrilled and energized by it that you're going to be changed, you're going to want to repudiate generalized negative thinking, and if you hear other people talking about negative thinking and pessimistic stuff and wasteful stuff, you're not going to want to be around them.   What I'm saying, if you hear your own voice in your mind and you're observing your mind complaining and trying to justify and blame and seek all this stuff, you're going to tell it to stop. You're going to want to wake up alive and on the right side of the bed and in tune with the infinite and connected to the world, and you're going to want to wake up and see the beauty of life, and regardless of what bad things happen.

And if you're anything like me or most people in general, we have all had some big challenges.....   I've gone through tragedies like Hurricane Katrina. I've lost loved ones, including my father. I've lost businesses, had people steal lots from me, and I've had burdens just like everyone else. I've had losses and defeats and pain and real catastrophic events in my life, but when you achieve this aliveness and this consciousness of now, you know that you can move on and you can prevail and even go to greater heights regardless of what happens because you truly have yourself and you have your unity, your empowerment, and your earnest connection to the Spirit of the Universe.

Power of Past and Present

Historically, there are nuggets of truth that many do not know about the power of now. And, through my studies of ancient shamanism in different parts of Asia and Northern Europe, the ancient peoples really did believe that the now is manifested here both in logic and language. And, these Northern tribes believed in only a past and a non-past, and there's no future until you have acted. So, in essence what that means is that "the now creates the future", or the now is the future as a byproduct of the past and present action. So thus, every moment of thought and action becomes the future, the present, and the past which guides and determines a set of pre-destinies or outcomes with variables that may be enhanced by the mind, body, and spirit.

Spiritual Filling and Re-Charging

There is a field of potentiality in the spiritual vacuum, but mind must be organized and cleansed to have that force and pressure to be effectively applied. Thus, when we want to create a new opportunity or new destiny, we need to realize that we need to purge ourselves in one of 2ways: either that or forcefully fill ourselves with some new information or new good or new ideas to push out the old, or we need to empty and clear our mind and heart and then allow new ideas and good to enter. And, must realize that IN nothing IS something. What that means is nothing is a blank page of your day or your life, and in that vacuum of nothingness it acts like a magnet that is supercharged by intent. So, a blank piece of paper, for instance, in your mind, the picture screen of your mind can be charged with your intent. And, that can become something in the supernatural world of your mind. Furthermore, it is your consciousness or your I-am-ness, or your "is-ness" that creates your consciousness. But, it's also the co-creator and manifestor of your experience and your journey. So basically, your consciousness, or your is-ness, or your mindfulness creates and manifests your experience. So, your worldview or your mental view of the world creates your journey.

The Spiritual Power of Imagination

By: G Mentz, Esq.

This is a discussion of the imagination with a focus on the teachings of various self help legends such as: Ben Franklin, Marcus Aurelius, Sun Tzu, Emerson, Thoreau, Napoleon Hill, Thomas Troward, James Allen, Wallace Wattles, Norman Vincent Peale, Neville Goddard, and Charles Haanel.

The world is but a canvas to the imagination. ~ HENRY DAVID THOREAU

In the following steps, the beauty and power of the imagination is illuminated. The secrets of how to use imagination as a force for creation and greatness are shown below. Enjoy.

1. We must learn to imagine ourselves in the right state of consciousness, and we must present ideas to our deeper mind and allow our consciousness to accept the ideas.

2. We must learn to think and view the world from a state of consciousness.

3. We must begin to learn how to think from the "finish line", think from the result, or think in the essence of victory

4. Learn to think from a state of mind or a mindset of having and enjoying something

5. We must learn to be in the assumption of having and be able see and feel ourselves "as if" the thing has happened. Think "from" the destiny.

6. In many cases we can think about a desired result or a purpose and look at all of the things that would be true for that result to happen.

7. Imagine looking at a matrix or a mosaic of successful outcomes that would need to happen for the ideal or desire to be manifested.

8. Remember that determined imagination or thinking from the "endgame or result" is the beginning of all great manifestation.

Imagination is the true magic carpet. ~ NORMAN VINCENT PEALE

9. We must imagine ourselves in the feeling of the result fulfilled during our waking hours and before bedtime.

10.   We must create a dominant stream of thoughts which would be necessary to be that thing, be the energy of the desire, or to have that thing.

11.   This quality of imagination would give us the state of mind or the superior mindset of being into with the purpose or the desired result

12.   We can translate imagination and vision into being and becoming.

13.   Thinking from the place of purpose is an intense perception of the world of fulfilled desire.

14.   Thinking from a standpoint of the desired outcome is creative living.

15.   We must put the past into our history and allow our present thoughts to manifest a state of mind which have become a future reality.

16.   We have a purpose or find a purpose or seek a purpose we begin to cultivate the necessary hunger in relation to that purpose. That hunger will help continually cultivate the dominant thoughts and the state of mind and the mindset necessary to manifest a greater imagination and results.

17.   An imagination is not just limited to the senses of taste, feel, smell, sound or site. Imagination is something where you can close your eyes and see something that you would enjoy in your life and look at it and see the essence of it.

<u>"Imagination should be used, not to escape reality, but to create it." ~ Colin Wilson</u>

18.   For example, if you wanted to be a professional tennis player or a professional pianist, you would see the essence of that result, see yourself performing with crowds, see yourself winning championships, seeing yourself making execution of points or the excellent execution of musical abilities. Seeing yourself victoriously being paid, the type of compensation that is required for a professional.

19.   At some point, you will be able to master a state of consciousness where your dominant thoughts generally pertain towards the results that you desire. Those dominant thoughts would focus on sending you toward the direction of your goals.

20.   This brings us to the idea that your dominant thoughts basically consist of your inner self talk and how you talk to

yourself, and the visions, the patterns of the ideas that you see flowing through your consciousness.

21.	If you can seize control over your mind and your memory and directed in a constructive way towards what you want, then you have effectively seized control of your dominant thinking.

Everything you can imagine is real.~ PABLO PICASSO

22.	The real key is to align your mind and your memory and align your inner character and your goals with each other.

23.	Accordingly, when great people say you have to "become that thing" that you want, that means aligning your energy, aligning your vibration, aligning your thinking, & aligning your skills in your mind with that result that you seek.

24.	As such, when the inner and outer worlds match each other is how reality is created.

25.	Some teachers talk about using a trance state or a hypnotic state to push imagination and ideas into the deeper consciousness. The ancient shamans called it Utiseta or "sitting out" which is an exercise where you are able to be in a " clear and peaceful state of mind" with no distractions and you are able to concentrate your mind on things that you want so as to use your imagination in a very vital and constructive way.

26.	When your imagination is so vivid and vital that it becomes real to you. You could sense it. You could touch it. You can do exercises with yourself where you see yourself in a particular situation where you can physically and mentally and emotionally feel the joy of that thing or that essence of being who you want to become. The idea is using your imagination to be, do and have what you want.

"Live out of your imagination, not your history." ~ Stephen R. Covey

27.   Generally some experts talk about how you must become fascinated or intrigued with what you really want. Using your imagination to see and feel happy about something you love. Something that you want to become dedicated and committed to.

28.   It's something that you think about happily and you look forward to. It is the harmonious and positive imagination regarding "what you want" that binds you to it. It creates a pleasant binding effect every time you imagine something with positive feeling,

29.   You are binding, imagining and aligning yourself with what you desire.

30.   The key with aligning yourself is so that your mind is not divided. They always say you don't want a divided house. Similarly, we don't want a divided mind neither. You want your mind, both sides of your mind and your heart and your soul cooperating with each other.

31.   To unify your mental house, sometimes that requires you to weed out the garden as they say and remove some of the anger or the resentment or the prideful emotions that you may have that are connected to something and allow those things to be purged and let go of your mind.

32.　　You purify yourself so you can have a more clear and emptier space in your heart in your mind to allow for your imagination to grow effectively and to become aligned with who and what you want to be and what you want to have be and do.

33.　　While all desires and results require action, the action begins in your mind and your imagination. There are many great Olympic sportsman or warriors with the military who rehearse every particular event in their mission plans and make sure they understand each task or point from beginning to end. They rehearse what needs to be done in their imagination. Also with this mental and physical practice, it helps winners get in the mindset of being aligned with and receptive to what they want to have.

"The best use of imagination is creativity." ~ Deepak Chopra

34.　　You have to center your imagination in the fulfilled desire with complete awareness and sensitiveness. This imagination can initiate optimal rewiring of neural pathways of your inner world.

35.　　Sometimes to begin something new and to begin something great, we must allow the old self to die out. The old personality or the old habits can be put aside so we can change our worldview, change our attitudes, change our habits, and change our heart.

36.　　We can become a new and open person where we can allow our deeper selves to have what we really, really want.

37.   Sometimes this may require us to rewrite or overwrite the past and sometimes it may require us to review our mindset and look at our memory of certain events and purge them.

38.   If it is something that you feel that you were wronged or something that you feel angry resentful about, sometimes you may be required to take that situation and look at it for what you learned about life or what lessons you learned from that situation

39.   Even in bad experience, every time something has happened negative in our life, there is a seed of power victory. There is a seed of lessons in that we never have to repeat those particular situations again, can avoid problem, and overcome obstacles that most people can't deal with.

40.   To become renewed and seek new greatness, there will be time where we have to allow ourselves to release old anger, destructive habits, or release resentment because we want to be able to purge the mental garbage.

41.   If we can't forgive, we may need to just let the rubbish go so we can move on.

The man who has no imagination has no wings. ~ MUHAMMAD ALI

42.   We do not want to waste time and be at war with ourselves and nobody wants unnecessarily relive past events in our minds.

43.   We need to remember that the quality of our "frame of mind" and the purity of your mindset is extremely important.

44.	Achieving optimal mind sometimes requires us to forgive and forget but mainly to quit wasting time harping on things, to quit revisiting events in our mind.

45.	Sometimes it's easier to fill the mind rather than just empty it. I remember a great class many years ago where a teach had dirty water in a glass bowl. He then took a hose and started pouring clean water into the dirty bowl of water and it was overflowing at the top. After about five minutes the water was clear in the bowl.

46.	So the point is, is there is two ways to renew and cleanse the consciousness. There is <u>emptying</u> and then there is <u>filling</u>. The key to this exercise is that filling yourself with things that are exciting makes you feel alive and filling your mind with ideas and events you are interested in and are fascinated with changes our attitudes and beliefs.

47.	By that active filling you are releasing and purging, overwriting and pushing out the types of messages and patterns and habits of thinking that are not useful to you.

48.	The Key point here is working to control your dominant self talk. If you increase dominant self talk in a certain area that are constructive and positive and uplifting, at some point your mind or your mindset or your vibration will become persuaded. It will be changed. It will be improved but it will be persuaded with new types of beliefs that will have overwritten the mental state or even the neurons that fire in your brain. They will fire differently after they are trained to fire in certain ways with regard to what you are more interested in and what you are you are more passionate about.

"The possible's slow fuse is lit by the imagination." ~ Emily Dickinson

49.   Over time your inner speech, that dominant speech, that pattern over time will be like a new weaving a certain type of threads into a garment. Over time the garment becomes what you are thinking about. More and more over time, the garment looks like the new types of thoughts and the types of habits and thinking that you have woven into the fabric of your life.

50.   So again in your thinking, we need to observe our inner speech, observe our dominant thoughts and observe those patterns. Because the thoughts that we have, if we pick certain thoughts and certain symbols and certain images in our imagination, we begin to attach certain symbols and certain words and certain ideas to what we want.

51.   So we are attaching our inner ideas and binding them towards our vision and our purpose to augment our worldview and our awareness is what it does.

52.   Remember many times when you change your worldview or you change your attitudes, you expand your awareness in the process. So let's just say for instance you have a new idea and your new idea is to get a certain type of clothing or a certain type of car, or golf clubs. Your awareness of those new ideas and things becomes heightened. Your awareness of the ideas or dreams that you desire to accomplish is clearer and the path become more reasonable.

53.   When you focus on something, even your awareness of the actual thing becomes heightened. Everybody knows if you buy a certain computer or a certain phone or a certain car, as soon as you have that thing you actually will start noticing others who actually have that type of car. More often you will

see that type of car on the street. You will notice your awareness is much higher because you know what that thing is. You understand what that thing is.

"I found I could say things with color and shapes that I couldn't say any other way–things I had no words for." - Georgia O'Keefe, Painter

54.	That's one of the keys with imagination and dominant thoughts along with inner speech. The secret is whatever it is that you want to become, you start to know what that is. You study it, you know what it is on the inside and the outside. You know what the essence or benefits of that thing is. You know what it does. You know how it works. You know the actual dynamics or specs of that thing. That's why again they say to receive something you have to become it or become in alignment with it or match it in energy.

55.	When you know what something is, you recognize it easier. In actuality your mindset needs to be of a harmonious mindset because only those that are harmonious find harmony and they never have to seek for it.

56.	The people that become harmonious attract harmony.

57.	This is just another reason why over the last hundred years, affirmations have become so popular. Prayers and petitions over the last 3000 years have been very popular. Mantras, spiritual poetry, prayers, psalms or repetitious types of readings where you either read or chant something out loud or in silence have been used for millennia .

58.	All these practices of speaking and praying your petitions or incantations are said to help change your mindset, to help change your worldview and it also change your vibration in the way you see things.

59.   It can be said that speech is the objectification of the images and the symbols and actions or the reverse of that is images and symbols and actions actually can become your inner speech. They are intertwined backwards and forwards.

"The future belongs to those who believe in the beauty of their dreams." -Eleanor Roosevelt, Politician

60.   Remember we need to find our chief aim and purpose. We need to find that desire or goal that we really want and can easily persuade ourselves to accept. Something that we can believe that we are worthy of, something that we can see as our potentiality.

61.   Then we need to align with it in both action and speech. Align with our desire, align with our purpose. The right to inner speech is essential.

62.   Even if you think about the ancient teachings from the East where they talk about virtuous: speech and mind and awareness. Right speech. Right mind. Right awareness.

63.   If you confuse your inner talk in your mind with your outer talk there will be conflict. We need to bring them in alignment with each other and then your actions, tasks, and abilities will manifest much more quickly toward our potential.

64.   Generally speaking we are in control of our thought and we are the cause of our inner mental discussion.

65.   Now if we seek inspiration, that is a different process of seeking ideas and a stream of thought from the Universe, but

your typical daily self talk is another thing. If you activate your inner receptivity, innovative thoughts can come from the universe. Like Edison and Einstein, both would take naps or rest to seek out solutions to problems.

66.   So alignment is key but what is also vital is cultivating gratitude and feeling. It is powerful to feel grateful for what is going on in your life now. Becoming thankful for your actions and your thinking now.

67.   Choose positive thoughts in relation to what you want.

68.   We have to assume the essence of being what we want to be. I mentioned that once before and I will mention it again that we have to assume the essence.   Here is an example of Essence: So if you want to complete a marathon, you have to see yourself going through it. See yourself going through every part of that race with all the different turns and twists and knowing how much time there will be left at a certain point. Then at the end of the marathon, see yourself completing it and finishing the achievement in a healthy and happy way is your ESSENCE.

69.   You can learn to pre-feel the "essence of being" a winner and essence of being a finisher of that particular event for example.

70.   Review and remember your actions. Reflect in your imagination on what you have done well each day and things you may not have excelled upon. Be determined to be better and do the right thing. Over 200 years ago, Ben Franklin worked his "precepts of order" each evening. He wanted to be excellent and build his character even at a mature age. Practice imagining yourself doing something with excellence and being your best to your loved ones, in your work, or even

imagine excellence with your creative or competitive future events.

71.   Considering all of this, every thought that we have, every action that we have, every omission that we have, those things we have in the now are creating our now-ness but they are also weaving our future.

72.   Create your inner speech in a way that blesses your life and others. Your inner speech should bless your health, happiness, love and prosperity.

Perhaps the real trouble was our almost total inability to point imagination toward the right objectives. Twelve Steps and Twelve Traditions, Bill W., Step Eleven, p.100

73.   This may sound oversimplified but we have to make our inner speech blessed and create a flow of good information and good reports. By choosing good things to focus on, this focus forms and inner sense of gratitude, of grateful sense of self talk.

74.   Thus, a Habitual or Habit of consciousness directed upon what we want with a vivid imagination pertaining to it, this clarifies and codifies our energy to manifest our desires.

75.   So with each goal we have a choice and when we make that choice we have to decide whether or not we are going to accept it. When we accept something, it can become a belief or an assumed future belief.

76.   So we are at a point where we are learning to fill ourselves, fill our hearts with the correct information,

vibrations, and energy. Fill our minds with dominant ideas and dominant thoughts and dominant speech or inner self talk related to harmony, quality of life that we want.

77.   We need to allow the excellent seed to flourish in our mental garden, and allow the bad seed of the garden really to wither, to be "pushed out" or to die out on its own. All of the unneeded ideas can be overcome with new and powerful ideas that are so strong that the constructive thought will push out from your mind what it is that is holding you back.

78.   In the end, we learn to accomplish these exercises of mind and memory, self talk, and actions/omissions. When all of these things become aligned with each other towards the goals that we want to achieve success can blossom. Our alignment will be towards the happiness we want our lives, towards the health we want in our lives.

79.   Most importantly, we need to identify with the new consciousness. We need to identify with that gratifying consciousness of what we want to be.

80.   So you have to identify with the consciousness of prosperity, love, and harmony. Identify with the consciousness of health. Identify with the consciousness of wealth. All of these things are your consciousness including happiness, health, wealth, worthiness, peace of mind, love. All of these qualities are the most important attributes for bliss and a magnificent recipe for success.

81.   Remember you have to give yourself consent to allow a new mindset to build within your subconscious mind.

82.   I think that's one of the most challenging things about changing attitudes, changing mindset, changing the way we act is one obstacle.   This one obstacle is putting aside

wishful-hope and allowing for ourselves to actually and finally change our deeply held beliefs.

83.   We have to give ourselves consent, a mental consent and accept aspiration and authentic change.

"Anything you may hold firmly in your imagination can be yours." "Our view of the world is truly shaped by what we decide to hear." ~ William James "Father of American Psyciology"

84.   I truly believe that all of these concepts herein form the basis of "liberation spirituality" because you don't have to depend on anybody else for anything. When you become in alignment with yourself and the universe, people, places and things will begin to act in accordance with your harmonious goals. Goals that don't hurt anybody but goals that would help you and other people. Help you serve humanity in a greater way. This is what I mean by liberation spirituality. Each individual could become a greater person and exercise their talents and serve humanity with helping others with the solutions they may need in their life or becoming the best you can be on a competitive level too.

85.   So to rehash, it is important to learn how to shut out all non productive ideas and divisive seeds in our minds. Shut those things out that interfere with our vision and our purpose and our goals.

86.   Learn to adjust our beliefs and put them at the forefront of our thinking in alignment with our desires and our purpose so as to activate the manifestation of the results what we seek.

87.   To do these things we would fuse ourselves with our purpose and become at one with our purpose. Just like an actor gets into the role and mind of the character.

88.   You could have many purposes. You should make yourself strong and great first for the benefit of yourself and all loved ones.

89.   Your purpose may be helping other people find their path. It could be helping someone become physically healthy. It could be helping someone learn something because you are a teacher or an instructor. It could be any one of those things.

Active imagination requires a state of reverie, half-way between sleep and waking. Without this playing with fantasy no creative work has ever yet come to birth. The debt we owe to the play of the imagination is incalculable. ~ Carl Jung - "Father of Modern Analytical Psychology"

90.   So we have to learn how to choose our state of being, choose our state of consciousness and imagine the receipt of your GOOD on a daily basis. Imagine ourselves in receipt of the essence and benefits of our desires. We have to learn to think from that place of joy and aliveness. Thing from the standpoint of having what we desire. Think from a place of what we will be able to be, have or do. It is only the ideals from which you think that our lives are realized. Your thought creates opportunity, a mindset, and a consciousness.

91.   In this new consciousness, you will have heightened abilities of: awareness, mindfulness, productivity, effectiveness, thought, speech and clarity.

92.   If you are having trouble at any time changing your mindset or breaking out of a mindset that you are stuck in, you need to find a thought or memory that you have that brightened your mood. Something from the past that you can latch onto mentally. Your victorious scene or your "peaceful scene" or your "successful scene" that you can picture in your imagination. You can train yourself to go back to that scene and imagine it "at will", and that will give you peace. With that piece of mind you are able to refocus and re-concentrate and what it is you want.

Conclusion

Remember this isn't about having perfect consciousness or having a perfect mindset that is directed towards your goal. It's really about getting your mindset over 50% clear and productive. Once you have a PMV positive mental vibration of over 50% most all of the time, you will be ahead of the vast majority of all people. You can now have a clear mental vibration of success, health, wealth, wholeness, worthiness, receptiveness, and aliveness. Once you allow yourself to get above 50%, the rewired consciousness takes over. The constructive mindset takes over as 51% of anything is greater than the rest and will color all else in it's vicinity. It's a majority and it takes over the entire mindset and that's the key.

The Philosophy of Wealth, Greatness, Health

The Philosophy of Wealth – The Philosophical Creed

There is a spiritual energy and force in every thought, from which all things are made, and which, in its original state, permeates, penetrates, and fills the interspaces of the Universe. A thought in this substance produces the thing that is imaged by the thought. Persons can form things in their thought, and by impressing their thoughts upon formless substance (interspaces of the Universe) can cause the thing he they think about to be created. In order to do this, people must pass from the competitive to the creative mind. Otherwise they cannot be in harmony with formless intelligence, which is always creative and never competitive in Spirit. *i.e. Being for the Creation of something and against nothing.*

People may come into full harmony with the formless substance by entertaining a lively and sincere gratitude for the blessings it bestows upon them. Gratitude unifies the mind of man with the intelligence of substance, so that man's thoughts are received by the formless. People can remain upon the creative plane only by uniting themselves with the formless intelligence through a deep and continuous feeling of gratitude. People must form a clear and definite mental image of the things they want to have, to do, or to become, and they must hold this mental image in their thoughts while being deeply grateful to the supreme that all their desires are granted. People who desire abundance must spend their leisure hours in contemplating their vision, and in earnest thanksgiving that the reality is being given to them.

Too much stress cannot be laid on the importance of frequent contemplation of the mental image, coupled with unwavering faith and devout gratitude. This is the process by which the impression is given to the formless and the creative forces set in motion. The clear and defined image can be sent into the universe as a confident petition for help. We should know how we will use the resulting abundance and understand the essence of how the prosperity will be used.

The creative energy works through the established channels of natural growth, and of the industrial and social order. All that is included in his mental image will surely be brought to people who follow the instructions given above, and whose faith does not waver. What they want will come to them through the ways of established trade and commerce. In order to receive their supply when it is ready to come to them, people must be in action in a way that causes them to more than fill their present place. They must keep in mind the clear purpose of prosperity through emotionalized realization of their mental image. And they must do, every day, all which can be done that day, taking care to do each act in a successful manner. They must give to every person a use value in excess of the value they receive, so that each transaction makes for more life, and they must hold the advancing thought so that the impression of increase will be communicated to all with whom they comes into contact.

The men and women who practice the foregoing instructions will certainly achieve abundance, and the riches they receive will be in exact proportion to the definiteness of their vision, the fixity of their purpose, the steadiness of their faith, and the depth of their gratitude. *Wallace D. Wattles (1910) – Enhanced by Prof. Mentz*

The Philosophy of Greatness

We are made of the one intelligent substance, and therefore all contain the same essential powers and possibilities. Greatness is equally inherent each unique individual, and may be manifested by all. Every person may become great. Many of the highest constituents of the Supreme Intelligence are also the constituents of man. We must learn to tap into these unused and latent spiritual powers. We may overcome both heredity and circumstances by exercising the inherent creative power of the soul. If we are to become great, the soul must act, and must rule the mind and the body over the simple ego thoughts. Our knowledge is limited, and we fall into error through spiritual ignorance. To avoid this illusion and unawareness, we must connect our soul with Universal Spirit. Universal Spirit is the intelligent substance from which all things come. It is in and through all things. All things are known to this universal mind, and we can so unite ourselves with it as to enter into spirit and higher knowledge. To do this we must cast out of ourselves everything that separates us from the Supreme. We must have sheer willingness to live the divine and abundant life, and we must rise above all simple, trivial, & moral temptations. The seeker of spiritual abundance must forsake, repudiate, or transcend every course of action that is not in accord with our highest ideals. We must reach the right viewpoint, recognizing that God is all, in all, and that there is nothing wrong. We must see that nature, society, government, and industry are perfect in their present stage, and advancing toward completion; and that all men and women everywhere are good and perfect while each on their own journey. We must know that all is right with OUR world, and unite with the Supreme for the engagement of perfect expression & work. It is only as we see the Universal Spirit as the Great Advancing Presence in all and see the good in all, that we can shift our consciousness to real greatness.   The seeker must consecrate themselves to the service of the highest that is within, obeying the voice of their heart and spirit. There is an Inner Light in everyone that continuously impels us toward the highest, and we must be guided by this light if we would become great. We must recognize the fact that we are one with the Supreme, and consciously affirm this unity for ourselves and for all others. We must know ourselves to be a "child of God" among "children of God", and act accordingly. We must have absolute faith in our own perceptions of truth, and begin at home to act upon these perceptions.   As we see the true and right course in small things and actions, we must take that course. We must cease to act unthinkingly, and begin to think; and we must be sincere and honest in our thought. We must form a mental conception of ourselves at the highest, and hold this conception until it is our habitual thought-form of ourselves. This thought-form we must keep continuously in view. We must outwardly realize and express that thought-form in our actions. We must do everything that we do in a great way. In dealing with our family, neighbors, acquaintances, and friends, we must make every act an expression of our ideals or highest good.   The person who reaches the right viewpoint and makes this full consecration, and who fully idealizes their self as great, and who makes every act, however trivial, an expression of the ideal, has already attained to greatness. Everything we do will be done in a great way. We will inherently make ourselves known by our good work and thinking, and will be recognized as a personality of power. We will receive knowledge by inspiration, and will know all that we need to know. We will benefit from and receive all the wealth we form in our thoughts, and will not lack for any good thing. We will be given ability to deal with any combination of circumstances that may arise, and our growth and progress will be continuous and rapid. [iii]

A Spiritual Exercise for Health.

A Spiritual exercise is a simple metaphysical methodology, not just in repeating words, but in the thinking of certain thoughts. Allowing these thoughts to permeate your being and sense and feel the thoughts will eventually allow them to become part of you. The words that we repeatedly say and hear become convictions. As Goethe says, the thoughts that we repeatedly think become habitual, and make us what we are. Moreover, Goethe implied that thoughts intertwined with character will enhance our action and boldness. The purpose in taking a mental exercise is that you may think certain thoughts repeatedly until you form a habit of thinking them, then they will be your thoughts all the time.

Taken in the right way and with an understanding of their purpose, mental and Spiritual exercises are of great value. The thoughts embodied in the following exercise are the ones you want to think. You should take the exercise once or twice daily, but you should muse over the thoughts continuously. That is, do not think them twice a day for a stated time and then forget them until it is time to take the exercise again. The exercise is to impress you with the formulation for continuous thought. Take a time when you can have from twenty minutes to half an hour secure from interruption and proceed first to make yourself physically comfortable. Rest at ease in a recliner, chair, bed, or on a couch; it is best to lie flat on your back. If you have no other time, take the exercise on going to bed at night and before rising in the morning. First let your attention travel over your body from the crown of your head to the soles of your feet, relaxing every muscle as you go. Relax completely.

And next, get physical and other ills off your mind. Let attention pass down the spinal cord and out over the nerves to the extremities, and as you do so think to yourself: My nerves are in perfect order all over my body. They obey my will, and I have great nerve force.   Next bring your attention to the lungs and think: I am breathing deeply and quietly, and the air goes into every cell of my lungs, which are in perfect condition. My blood is purified and made clean.   Next, to the heart: My heart is beating strongly and steadily, and my circulation is perfect, even to the extremities. Next, to the digestive system: My stomach and bowels perform their work perfectly. My food is digested and assimilated and my body rebuilt and nourished. My liver, kidneys, and bladder each perform their several functions without pain or strain; I am perfectly well. My body is resting, my mind is quiet, and my soul is at peace. I have no anxiety about financial or other matters. God, who is within me, is also in all things I want, impelling the highest good toward me; all that I want is already given to me. I have no anxiety about my health, for I am perfectly well. I have no worry or fear whatever. I rise above all temptation of moral evil. I cast out all greed, selfishness, and narrow personal ambition; I do not hold envy, malice, or enmity toward any living soul. I will follow no course of action that is not in accord with my highest ideals. I am right and I will do right. [iv]

KEEPING THE HIGHEST HEALTH VIEWPOINT WITHIN AND WITHOUT

All is right with the world. It is perfect and advancing to completion. I will contemplate the facts of social, political, and industrial life only from this high viewpoint. Behold, life and the world is all very good. I will see all human beings, all my acquaintances, friends, neighbors, and the members of my own household in the same way. They are all good. Nothing is wrong with the Universe or my world; nothing can be wrong but my own personal attitude, and henceforth I keep that right. My whole trust is in the Supreme Master.

CONSECRATION OF HEALTH

I will obey my Inner Spirit and be true to what within me is highest. I will search within for the pure idea of right and good in all things, and when I find it I will express it in my outward life. I will abandon everything I have outgrown for the best I can think. I will have the highest thoughts concerning all my relationships, and my manner, character, and action shall express these thoughts inwardly and outwardly. I will surrender my body to be ruled by my mind; I yield my mind to the dominion of my higher source, and I give my soul to the guidance of my higher power.

IDENTIFICATION & RECOGNITION OF HEALTH

There is but one substance and source, and of that I am made and with it I am one. It is my Father; I proceeded forth and came from it. My Father and I are one, and my Father is greater than I, and I do His will. I surrender myself to conscious unity with Pure Spirit;

there is but one and that one is everywhere. I am one with the Eternal Consciousness.

IDEALIZATION OF HEALTH

Form a mental picture of yourself as you want to be, and at the greatest height your imagination can picture. Dwell upon this for some little time, holding the thought: "This is what I really am; it is a picture of my own perfect and advancing to completion. I will contemplate the facts of social, political, and industrial life only from this high viewpoint. Behold, it is all very good. I will see all human beings, all my acquaintances, friends, neighbors, and the members of my own household in the same way. They are all good.

Nothing is wrong with the universe, nothing can he wrong but my own personal attitude, and henceforth I keep that right. My whole trust is in God.

REALIZATION OF HEALTH

I appropriate to myself the power to become what I want to be, and to do what I want to do. I exercise creative energy; all the power there is, is mine. I will arise and go forth with power and perfect confidence; I will do mighty works in the strength of the Lord, my God. I will trust and not fear, for God is with me. [v]

- Remember that simple pains and discomforts are sometimes signals to take action to better your physical health; however, many pains are the body at work healing and regenerating itself on a cellular and molecular level.

- As a note, you may be able to work this positive person in your MIND for other people.

[vi] *Wallace Wattles (1910) Enhanced by Prof. Mentz*

Philosophy of Gratitude

To convey the idea of your wants to the universe, it becomes necessary to relate yourself to the formless intelligence in a harmonious way.

To secure this harmonious relation is a matter of such primary and vital importance that I shall give some space to its discussion here and give you instructions which, if you will follow them, will be certain to bring you into perfect unity of mind with the Supreme Power, or God.

The whole process of mental adjustment and attunement can be summed up in one word: <u>Gratitude</u>.

First, you believe that there is one intelligent substance, from which all things proceed. Second, you believe that this substance gives you everything you desire. And third, you relate yourself to it by a feeling of deep and profound gratitude.

Many people who order their lives rightly in all other ways are kept in poverty by their lack of gratitude. Having received one gift from God, they cut the wires which connect them with the Supreme by failing to make acknowledgment.

It is easy to understand that the nearer we live to the source of wealth, the more wealth we shall receive, and it is easy also to understand that the soul that is always grateful lives in closer touch with God than the one which never looks to the SUPREME in thankful acknowledgment. The more gratefully we fix our minds on the supreme when good things come to us, the more good things we will receive, and the more rapidly they will come. And the reason simply is that the mental attitude of gratitude draws the mind into closer touch with the source from which the blessings come.

If it is a new thought to you that gratitude brings your whole mind into closer harmony with the creative energies of the universe, consider it well, and you will see that it is true. The good things you have already have come to you along the line of obedience to certain laws. Gratitude will lead your mind out along the ways by which things come, and it will keep you in close harmony with creative thought and prevent you from falling into competitive thought.

Gratitude alone can keep you looking toward the all, and prevent you from falling into the error of thinking of the supply as limited — and to do that would be fatal to your hopes.

There is a law of gratitude, and it is absolutely necessary that you should observe the law if you are to get the results you seek. The law of gratitude is the natural principle that action and reaction are always equal and in opposite directions.

The grateful outreaching of your mind in thankful praise to the Supreme intelligence is a liberation or expenditure of force. It cannot fail to reach that to which it addressed, and the reaction is an instantaneous movement toward you.

"Draw nigh unto God, and he will draw nigh unto you." That is a statement of psychological truth. And if your gratitude is strong and constant, the reaction in formless substance will be strong and continuous; the movement of the things you want will be always toward you. Notice the grateful attitude that Jesus took, how he always seems to be saying, "I thank thee, Father, that thou hearest me." You cannot exercise much power without gratitude, for it is gratitude that keeps you connected with power. But the value of gratitude does not consist solely in getting you more blessings in the future. Without gratitude you cannot long keep from dissatisfied thought regarding things as they are.

The moment you permit your mind to dwell with dissatisfaction upon things as they are, you begin to lose ground. You fix attention upon the common, the ordinary, the poor, the squalid, and the mean — and your mind takes the form of these things. Then you will transmit these forms or mental images to the formless. And the common, the poor, the squalid, and the mean will come to you.

To permit your mind to dwell upon the inferior is to become inferior and to surround yourself with inferior things. On the other hand, to fix your attention on the best is to surround yourself with the best, and to become the best. The creative power within us makes us into the image of that to which we give our attention. We are of thinking substance, too, and thinking substance always takes the form of that which it thinks about.

The grateful mind is constantly fixed upon the best. Therefore it tends to become the best. It takes the form or character of the best, and will receive the best. Also, faith is born of gratitude. The grateful mind continually expects good things, and expectation becomes faith. The reaction of gratitude upon one's own mind produces faith, and every outgoing wave of grateful thanksgiving increases faith. The person who has no feeling of gratitude cannot long retain a living faith, and without a living faith you cannot attain true prosperity by the creative method.

It is necessary, then, to cultivate the habit of being grateful for every good thing that comes to you and to give thanks continuously. And because all things have contributed to your advancement, you should include all things in your gratitude.   Do not waste a lot of time thinking or talking about the shortcomings or wrong actions of those in power. Their organization of the world has created your opportunity; all you get really comes to you because of them. Do not rage against corrupt politicians. If it were not for politicians we should fall into anarchy and your opportunity would be greatly lessened.

The Supreme Intelligence has worked a long time and very patiently to bring us up to where we are in industry and government, and he is going right on with his work. There is not the least doubt that he will do away with plutocrats, trust magnates, captains of industry, and politicians as soon as they can be spared, but in the meantime, they are all very necessary. Remember that they are all helping to arrange the lines of transmission along which your riches will come to you, and be grateful. This will bring you into harmonious relations with the good in everything, and the good in everything will move toward you. [vii]

Exercises for Concentration, Meditation, and Energy

Concentration Exercise

1. Find a relaxed part of your home

2. Sit and quiet the mind and begin to relax each part of the body (that you can think of) from head to toes.

3. Shut your eyes & take a few deep breaths.

4. Think of a room that you lived in as a child or that you are presently in.

5. Begin to see and visualized in your mind the entire room and its contents and where things are located. (Whatever you can recall)

6. It is also good to imagine the exact color of things in the room with your eyes closed.

7. This is also a good exercise to do even after you have entered a new building or place.

8. Do this for a few minutes each day and your focus and concentration will increase. These days, there is computer software that actually runs programs to help concentration in this same way..

9. As a note, this same type of exercise is also very good to relax and vividly recall wonderful people or possessions that you have in your past or present.

- Open your eyes when done with any of these exercises ☺

Active Meditation Exercise

1. Engage steps 1, 2 & 3 above.
2. With eyes closed and imagining, see yourself going into a sacred castle.
3. As you enter the main chamber, you see the (helpful person of your choice).
4. This person could be alive or from the past.
5. You then discuss with her or him in your minds eye. [imagination]
6. You ask questions and your Friendly Guru answers these questions.
7. Try and sense the answers from your core (heart and stomach).
8. When you are finished, thank your friend for the help and guidance.
9. You may have an overwhelming sense that this voice or person is from a higher or different viewpoint than your own.

Exercise for Energizing or Healing Yourself.

1) Engage steps 1,2, and 3 above. (Relaxing in a chair with spine straight) relax your hands on your lap.

2) Close your eyes and visualize a peaceful lake that has no ripples. Then see yourself surrounded by bright white particles of energy that also permeates your body.

3) In your mind, see the bright light move toward and focus on the area of discomfort or pain. Allow this white light to fill any affected area and flow thought your body.

4) Know that the white light brings all of your body's healing power to work most effectively for you.

5) Take a few breaths.

6) Then, allow this bright light to act like water and flow though your body.

7) Allow the "fluid of light" purify and wash your entire body.

8) Feel and see in your minds eye that the washing fluid of white light is "pure love" and cleanses you of ANY AND ALL fear, resentment, hurt, and dis-ease.

9) Say to yourself, I forgive myself and everyone for the past.

   Thank the light of the universe for removing any impurities from your body.

10) Claim mental freedom from all problems in your mind and spirit. Thank the universe for your health and peace.

11) See others in your mind's eye walking up to you and congratulating you on your healing and success.

12) That's it….. & Open your eyes.

Perception and Awareness Exercise

1. Sit is a relaxed position
2. Relax each part of the body and take a few deep breaths.
3. Imagine a warm energy radiating through your body.
4. Enter what we call the Alpha State – which is Relaxed Daydreaming and Right Brain.
5. Now, begin to feel or sense each part of the body.
6. Direct your attention to your toes or hands or ears.
7. Notice how each part of the body feels.
8. Now close your eyes and notice any sounds either of your body or around you.
9. See if you can hear something far away.
10. Now, refocus and imagine just one sound or image.
11. Focus all of your thought on seeing, hearing, feeling, or tasting/smelling only one thing that you imagine.
12. Imagine this one thing to the exclusion of everything else.
13. As an example, try to imagine just the sound of a soft trumpet or French horn playing a song.
14. After a few minutes, relax again and come back to your BETA state of mind and consciousness. Left Brain

Affirmation Exercises

1. Affirmations should be affirmative. Each affirmation can be written in an "AS IF" phrase or sentence.

2. Affirmations can be for health, success, peace, safety, relationships, or even supply in the form of money.

3. Affirmations can be said out loud or in silence. Some people love to do their affirmations in the mirror.

4. A prime example of an affirmation could be, " I am healthy, happy, successfully, loved and whole. I am part Supreme Intelligence and the Supreme only creates beauty and perfection."

5. Keep in mind, you should have an "essence in back of affirmations". As an example, a supply affirmation could say, "I will earn an extra 5000 dollars in the next 4 weeks by providing excellent service as a salesperson or expert or by effectively serving others...."

6. As you can see, the above affirmation specifies some distinct creative work and cooperation related to your prosperity, and it is not a blind or hopeful demand to receive something for nothing. You can always affirm mentally or out loud for possibilities and opportunities.

7. There are primary reasons against blind affirmations for things or money of which we will not discuss at length. However, if a person demands 100 thousand dollars from the supreme, it may come in the form of an injury settlement which might not be your first choice.

8. Overall, we should state our affirmations with confidence, love, harmony, gratitude, and faith. With this

combination, the universe will gladly begin working to unfold opportunities and blessings for you.

9. As such, a clear thought or idea that is repeated again and again is almost certain to manifest a replica of itself in the future. If the thought is held strongly, with gratitude and feeling, and in a creative way that does not hurt others, your desire will come quickly as the imagined formulation or something even better will unfold.

Prescience and Intuition

This section is about how to develop your intuition or our inspiration. First of all, what's the difference between inspiration and intuition? Well, let's say you start your morning with some meditation. You sit down and you read some meditative books. And, you ponder them and you muse over those ideas that you've read, that information that you've read. And, as you sit peacefully with your quiet mind, while ideas begin to flow to you about what you should do with your day, or some other concern in relation to the reading that you've had.

And, from those ideas you've received some inspiration which technically is a type of intuition. And, this information has come to you, and you need to decide how to act upon it. And, the best way to decide upon any intuition or any inspiration that you've received, an idea from the universe is to filter it through some simple ethical and virtuous principles such as: lovingness, and kindness, and is it pure and good for your mind, is it harmless to other people, is it good for you and other people, is it unselfish and is it loving. Those are just some basic principles that you should use.

Furthermore, the ideas should be backed by some facts so that the idea is a calculated risk but probable success. Thus, if the facts back up your idea, if you act upon the idea with action, belief, intent, planning, and hard work, the probability of success is good.

Practices of Seeking Prescience and Inspiration Consciousness.

1) Talk to Your Higher Self Exercise

One, you might want to go through a guided meditation or guided fantasy of sorts. You can imagine yourself going to a beautiful castle in the mountains, and you arrive there, and you walk into the hall of a beautiful castle room, and you see someone at the throne there, and low and behold, it's you. It's you, but it's the glorified, the wonderful you who's the king or queen of the castle. And, you go and speak directly to that person. You sit down next to them or in front of them or stand in front of them, and you ask questions. And, once you ask a question in your mind's eye, you wait for the answer and see what comes.

The magic of this mindful practice is that for many people another genuine tone of voice will RESPOND. It's an authentic voice different from yours, and it will give answers to your questions. Like should I take this job, or should I invest in this certain venture, should I be better friends with a certain person, or take the relationship to another level. These are just some basic examples. Or, should I move to a different place, or foreign land, etc.. The goal here is to make friends with your Higher Self and learn to seek the wisdom to the deeper and authentic self which knows your truth and the best answers for you.

2) Magic Door Exercise

The second practice or exercise is you go to the same castle in your mind where you go to a special room with a door. Then, you ask a question to yourself before you go to the door, and when the door opens, after you've asked the question, there's either going to be a yes or no in your mind when the door opens.

3) Divining Symbols

The third way might be to use a card or a rune or some type of decision piece, and you ask a question and you pick the card or the rune or the decision piece, and it can give you an answer, a yes or a no, or maybe, or something descriptive. There're various different types of decision type cards or runes, and each card might have a different response or a different opinion on it about what to do. That's just one example, or you can use an object to help you with your intuition.

4) Contemplative Object

The fourth practice is contemplative intuitive practice. This exercise would be to pick an object, maybe it could be a stain glass window or a beautiful picture. And, you focus on it for a while. The object could be a crystal or special rock. And, you observe it, and you look deeply at it, and you become receptive, and perceptive. And, you allow the feelings to come into you, and you allow the impressions and inspiration and ideas and intuition to flow to you. Doing this, you're somewhat in a trance state focusing on a particular object and nothing else, focusing on one object while avoiding all other things around you without distraction. And, that's the type of deep contemplation somewhat akin to Taizé meditation of the mystical Catholics. Almost all cultures have some type of iconic meditative practice.

5) Meditative Musing

And, number five would be just to read an affirmation or meditation and then to have some quiet time, and to allow thoughts and ideas and inspiration to come to you. I mentioned this before, but it could be a meditative book, or many people in different literatures have suggested that you just open a page in your favorite wisdom literature. It could be the Bible, Old Testament or New Testament. It could be some Native American, Vedic or Buddhist writings. It doesn't matter. And, you just open a page to it, you read it, and then meditate over that, and you allow, without distraction for your quiet time. To begin, it is sometimes best to take a few deep breaths, relaxed your body from head to toe, and you're able to go through this process of just allowing your mind to receive this beautiful information that comes from in and around the universe. With this practice you may have some aha moments from time to time which resolve long standing questions or challenges.

6) Look for Signs based on a Question

Number six, you can ask a question in the morning or in the evening, it doesn't matter. Let's say you ask a question in the morning of yourself like would it be good for me to move to Washington D.C., or London, it doesn't matter. And, you ask that question very quietly and very assertively to yourself in the morning in a relaxed way. And during that day, you look for signs. You look for signs and symbols from the universe that may guide you. And, let's say you're driving down the road that day, and you see a sign that says Washington or London or whatever it might be. Let's say that somebody starts talking about they had a great time while living at a certain place and you learn more. That's just an example of how you could ask a question and look for signs in your daily life.

7)   Pattern Writing

And number seven, you write out ideas or questions that come to you mind and you keep writing them out on a scrap of paper. Let's say you write out, should I take this job, or should I move to this place, or should I invest in this investment, and you write these things down, you just keep writing out what comes to your mind. It could be anything. And, as you write these things out, maybe you'll see a **pattern** in the writing. And, that pattern on that page may, the totality of the ideas may give you sign or a symbol or some path to take, or some way to act or not act. This may be especially effective with the type of work or hobbies that you seek. The overall pattern of ideas may point you to a type of work that you may master and become great at doing.

8)   Imagine Decisions in the Future

Another way to imagine doing something, a decision, imagine taking action in your life in some area, and then lock that idea in mentally and basically bring it down from your mind into your heart, almost like swallowing it, and feel this decision's impact on you and try to feel it in your heart, mind, and gut, but particularly in your gut.

So, you are imagine doing something like buying a house or a condo or a car, or moving to another place, or taking a job. You are imagining a new future event, you are imagining what it's like, imagining the outcome, and then you try to feel in your gut whether or not it is good or bad. Is it a yes or a no feeling?

And then you mentally turn on the computer in your mind and select the future time and date and result to see if the decision is beneficial or prevents harm, where it is not harmful. So, the key to this is really locking in some moment in the future, maybe a year from now, whatever, and just imagining what that future experience is like. It's got to be a little bit specific, but other than that, it's a good way to formulate the potentiality of a a yes or no feeling in your center of emotions and gut..

9) Object Holding Exercise – Sense the Energy

Another quick exercise would be maybe to hold an object that represents what the future might be and try and see if your imagination presents any ideas or events based on holding that object, whether you receive a little mental-movie clip or an idea that's running through your mind. This is yet another simple exercise to test your intuition or your inspiration.

10)   The Papal Bowl of Intuition Exercise

Another exercise would be to cut out a couple of slips of paper and write on each slip of paper a particular action that you might take, or an object that you want or a type of car, it doesn't matter, and you are just writing three or four ideas on pieces of paper. You are sticking them in a bowl and you allow maybe one of your children to pick something from the bowl or a trusted friend. This is an idea that's been around forever. Even some of the popes in foreign lands are picked this way. In Egypt, the pope is selected by, they put three names of three Bishops in a bowl, and they allow a small child to pick one of the names out of the bowl and that's how the Pope is selected in the Coptic Church in Egypt.

In sum, this is a very existential practice of knowing yourself and trying to be your best and basically existentialism is really the freedom that lies where your authentic self is discovered.

Summary of Ideas – A Parabolic Workbook to Success

In The Moment Intuition – Power of Inspiration

Wealth is a force for good, a force for learning, helps create experiences, funds expanded talents, and allows for expanded giving. In the essence of wealth, our reality is our acceptance of good. Success and prosperity and financial freedom is a reasonable option in life. Therefore, accepting the reasonableness and possibility of good in every moment is a present form or wealth consciousness.

Exercises to Harness Your Passions in Life

1. Take a moment to list the ideas that you have in the moment right now, and meditate on your objectives that you have. And then, listen to yourself and see what your thoughts are around your goals and objectives.

2. And then, mentally engage your idea, and then you can build upon the idea with action and allow innovation and improvisation.

3. What decision feels right? Use your gut without focusing on limited data. Change routines or do something differently, and empty yourself of your preconceptions.

4. What makes you feel alive? What is your passion? What would you do for free if you could do it?

5. How can you serve that will help the most people?

6. Earnestly commit to a full, free, and spiritual, and wealthy life.

7. Be good to yourself and know yourself and let go of your blocks and mental hindrances to your happiness.

8. Decide to believe and know that you can be what you want, do what you want and have what you want.

9. Define your mission. Who are you? What do you love to do? What do you want to be? What do you want to create? How will you serve? How will you create solutions for yourself and others?

10.   Itemize what you want. See yourself using all of it. See yourself using all of the good that comes to you – the essence of your rewards and how you will use them for yourself and other people.

11.   Empty yourself of mental thinking that keeps you from your dreams, and make room for growth, renewal.

12.   Refocus on what is right with your world. Grow, change, learn, expand, experience, every penny you spend should be on growth, health and productivity.

13.   Follow your heart, mind and soul, and take steps. Be aware and mindful, and use zeal in your life.

14.   Revitalize yourself and be aware and engage life. Try and transform yourself into a rebirth, allow renewal, let go of your old views, study new ideas, expand new perspectives, become reborn in life, be aware of abundance, see abundance, try to see it in everything.

15.   Develop a Prosperity Consciousness: See wealth, see prosperity, see beauty of nature, open your eyes to opportunity.

16.   If you are going to engage life, you're going to have to think big, use big ideas, and find big solutions.

17.   Action: And, once you have these big ideas, and solutions. You need to call people and act on these solutions, meet with others, communicate, connect to others

18.   Deals: Get the deals done that are necessary to put all it altogether, get past your fear, get out of your comfort zone. And if someone says no, kick the dust off your sandals and move onto the next person.

19.   Brand: You need to brand yourself and do all you can do to promote your ideas and solutions to the masses, and deliver the best and fastest service. If you can do all these things, you will be great.

Steps needed to Make Big Changes

1. The first would be desire.

2. Thought and imagery.

3. Open minded and awareness to change.

4. Planning.

5. Action.

6. Commitment to that action, and earnestness and sincerity.

7. Aim or what is your purpose.

8. Essence. The essence and what's in back of the purpose, such as emotions. And then how you devote your attention and what you are loyal to.

9. Remove or diffuse blocks and obstacles.

10.   Connecting with the animating source, and develop a harmonious relationship with the Life Force.

11.   Remaining grateful, thankful, and cultivate praise, both for yourself and other people.

12.   Be aware of abundance and opportunity and goodness, and how your consciousness in all of that in sum is how your consciousness controls your destiny.

Consciousness Exercises

Here are special observations for optimizing your consciousness. Consciousness through certain mental and physical, spiritual practices.

1. There is a collective consciousness and harmonic resonance, and how that affects the individual in their mind and memory. We have a stream of consciousness, and how that thought affects your consciousness in the 21st century, is the C2K. And then there is the spoken word and written word of effect in what you speak and what you write, and how that changes your consciousness going forward after you have made that mental imprint.   And then there is controlled visualization, or controlled hypnagogia.   Then there is autosuggestion, and how to use repetition in statements of affirmation and decrees to alter and enhance our ongoing mental stream of consciousness.

2. Our essence or being is altered by our thinking and your acting, and habits. Mindfulness, meditation and contemplation affects your consciousness. We can work at emptying or filling our mind with new information.

3. Then there are theories and ideas by greats such as Carl Jung who discussed archetypes and the imprints that are already within you, and what your types of passions, hobbies and work that you tend toward doing based on your archetype or what's in your background. In Vedic Hindu literature, there are many great writings about the energy of: purpose, dharma and even tapas.

4. One key exercise is to improve your consciousness through catharsis, purging, clearing, forgiving, cleansing of your mind and processing information, processing data. Just like a

computer processor which has a memory, hard drive and temporary files and cache. We all realize these things need to be optimized to work together.. The same is true with the consciousness, and then there is spiritual energy that animates mind, and how that affects you. How spirituality affects a person.

5. The next exercise would be we have to advance in the type, quality, and nature of our dominant conscious thoughts. We have a choice in the type, quality, and nature of the dominant conscious thoughts that we have, and how do we change our thinking and alter the choices of our thoughts.

6. As an example in Philippians 4 it talks about how to choose what is true and beautiful and right, righteous and so forth. And that is a conscious choice sometimes for many people where we use our power of: will or willingness to direct our thoughts to what is positive.

The Mind of Wonder and Awe

Awe and wonder are things that we perceive that are not typically in the five senses of taste, feel, smell, sound, and seeing, so we actually can experience something without a tangible comprehension. So, awe is also part of an extra-sensory perception, along with empathy as well. Since emotions are based on perception, there is something beyond the mere perception that causes a varying emotions.

The next section is about prayer and meditation, communing with the spirits and with God. A trance state, a meditative state, and the essence of the search for Maximum Peace/Awareness is to maximize consciousness of life, abundance, aliveness, potential, and awareness. If we can operate from a higher order of perception, our view and journey are optimized. Further, a higher consciousness allows a greater connection prescience, and imagination, which can be utilized upon our inner and outer worlds.   We have to be contemplative in action, and that is being connected to the universe, while being conscious of what is going on which, in essence, taps us into a higher grade of thought and insight.

In every culture there are different parts of the body from the crown at the top of your head to your heart to your throat down to your stomach and lower chakras and to your feet that ground you to the earth. All of these are interesting aspects of your body and yourself, which could be equated to aspects or facets of the soul as well.

Here is a short list of things or issues that may affect consciousness that may be beyond the normal 5 senses. Ways to alter consciousness and thinking.

1. There is the breath or the breath of life, and how the air itself you breath and the contents of that air can affect you and the quality of the air can affect you.

2. There are exercises and poses and different routines for the body to be stretched or strengthened.

3. There is nature and earth and how to commune with nature and the earth, whether it is outward bound or a vision quest, or anything else.

4. There are the five elements. How earth, wind, fire and ice, or a fifth element such as the all permeating ether that is in the interspaces of the universe.

5. The of course, diet and nutrition affects your consciousness and your perception of life.

6. There is also fellowship with others and whom you associate with, who you talk to, what you verbalize, what you hear and listen to—how that energy or vibration affects your consciousness.

7. Lists and objectives alter your consciousness. If you write a journal or make a list or add goals to the list, how does that change your focus and your intention, and how you put things in order in your life—the order in which they are important.

8. There are environmental issues, the people, the placed, and the things and the arrangement of energy and objects around you. Whether order changes your consciousness

9. The teacher and a guru relationship is an affect. If someone who is your trusted advisor, how does that affects your consciousness and your growth and your human potential.

10.   How you speak is an affect. Your incantations and decrees, and affirmations and what you say and what you repeat out loud or in prayer, how that would affect your mental consciousness.

11.   Applied meaning or your past. This raises the question of how your past or your childhood, and how your ancestors and elders all affects your karma, circumstances, luck, and your reaping and sowing of life.

12.   How you utilize imagination and how to use exercises of imagination to expand your consciousness.

13.   Neuroplasticity. Really about changing or reprogramming the way you think about your competencies.

14.   Nootropics. How nutrition and diet and supplements, herbs and other types of regulated intake of chemicals can affect your awareness, function, consciousness, whether they are holistic chemicals or not.

15.   Altered states; how some people are just born different. Some people were born really thinking in a vertical way or a horizontal way, and some people have visionary capacities, are more spatial in their mind. And some people who are a little on the edge of either autism or Asperger's or some type of bipolar issues. Sometimes those conditions can allow a person to think both logically, but more importantly in a non-logical way, which allows them to think outside of what the normal people are confined to.

16.   Inner Gravity? And then the last issue is just the inner ear. How the compass or gravity of your inner body can affect you, and what that is. Everyone has an inner ear situation where it could be adjusted if necessary.

Here are some steps that most people may find necessary to innovate, grow, expand, improve, or even heal.

1. A burning desire supported by real facts.
2. Repairing error thought – incorrect human beliefs about self and others.
3. Writing out or discussing what you really want to do with your life.
4. Humility and a willingness to listen and learn (teach-ability)
5. Ability to rise above the challenges & to forgive self and others
6. An ability to do what it takes to transcend above challenges.

7. A clear comprehension of the benefits of change, the sacrifices needed to transcend, and the pain associated lack of change.

8. Moving toward Natural Expression of what you life was meant to be.

Other points that groups such as EST and The Course in Miracles espouse are how we interpret the MEANING of the past. Also with the 12 steps, Mind Science, and therapeutic organizations, the issues of character analysis, making and discussing an inventory of past, and working through the details of your memories, experiences, fears and resentments are key to growth. Those who can take a hard look at themselves and experiences and learn from them are the people who can grow. Those who can look at one part of the past as an experience that does not totally define them will also grow. Those who can purge thoughts of anger, fear or resentment to obtain purity of thoughts and freedom of mind will have peace. In sum, a person who is willing to look at their part and involvement in the past, discuss it, and pray for release from the bond of the past will be liberated.

The 12 Step Philosophy that is credited to Bill Wilson and Dr. Bob Smith was quite innovative also. With the influences of people like Fr. Ed Dowling and Dr. Sam Shoemaker, the 12 steps suggest that you have a God of Your Own Understanding. Therefore, this method virtually eliminated dissent because each person could find their own unique God or Higher Power and develop a personal and direct relationship without a middleman. Those who simply can't get to the point of "God" or "Higher Power" Belief or observance are encouraged to allow the conscience of the group or the power of the principles/primary purpose to be their "Higher Power". GOD is said to not be a requirement for these programs to work effectively. Those who expand and improve their life are people who work the steps, tackle self-analysis & clean house, make room for good in their life, clear the wreckage of the past, engage prayer and meditation, help others, and grow spiritually. Invariably, all people who are successful are working spirituality in their life in one form or another. Sometimes there are self styled atheists that are successful, and most of them treat the steps or the group force as their "Higher Power". As such, even the Atheist must maintain sufficient humility and "connectedness" to remain successful. Therefore, all prosperous members must avoid "playing God" out of sheer necessity so that they may maintain and achieve peace and harmony.

Why do People Attend Retreats or Group Meetings?

Retreat based groups, Course in Miracles and 12 Step Based methodologies all take advantage of some of these factors also:

- To Unplug, Get Away, To find Calm or Peace, To Commune with Nature or People.

- To seek Interruption, Moment of Clarity, or Awakening – When someone is ready for change or spiritual or moral change is induced by confrontation.

- Character Development – Where higher standards of living and performance are aspired to.

- Building bridges instead of burning them – People are taught metaphysical systems to avoid large problems or eliminate/reduce past or present conflicts.

- Spreading the word i.e. teaching as part of learning and living a program which was also later revealed in Dr. S. Covey's research.

Boot Camp Seminars and Retreats – Purpose and Benefits

Many seminars and retreats are "so called" life changing engagements. Some of these seminars are designed to do several things:

- To unwind and unplug from the world with like minded people.

- To take time for self analysis, evaluate progress, and plan.

- To hear top speakers who address topics of interest on relationships, family, business or success.

- To be involved in interactive group learning and discussions.

- To interrupt the EGO and refocus on what is important.

- To learn to head toward your Natural Purpose or Expression.

- To have professionals confront and challenge the attendee regarding their thinking, actions or even insanity.

- Some retreats or seminars encourage "Group Guided Fantasy or Group Guided Recall" to help the attendee work through past experiences.

The Boot-Camp, Warrior Weekends, Life-Training, or Westernized Zen Master style retreats or seminars can help people develop a new awareness as to what is important. With the "in-your-face" teachings and contractual discipline, these courses tend to focus on breaking your pre-conceptions to open your mind. If the leaders can create a willingness for change, they may interrupt your thinking for a moment of crucial clarity. This clarity is desired by the leaders so that the postulant can muster a change in thought or find a "call to action or purpose" in their life.

Many of these courses may help people get an honest self appraisal of themselves. With skilled leaders, attendees may find exactly what is holding them back without holding on to blame. Others may learn to transcend victimhood and the desire for sympathy.

The overall goal of these training programs is to promote effectiveness and allow the breaking-through of mental barriers. By breaking through, you become free to live and take action via becoming responsible.

Learning how to accept life events, putting the past behind, & getting out of comfort zones are all major themes of these Carpe Diem focused organizations and teachings. If the candidate can become open to possibilities and learn to experience life and have

real experiences. Are you interpreting your life in constructive
ways? Another focus of these trainings would be discipline,
commitment, integrity and so on. Are you a man or woman of your
word. Do you do what you say you will do? Many of these
programs use empirical analysis of your track record. Thus, the
reality of your integrity score must be seen objectively. If the
candidate can be helped to look at their truth and history, the room
for improvement in their life can be great.

*Man can will nothing unless he has first understood that he
must count on no one but himself; that he is alone, abandoned
on earth in the midst of his infinite responsibilities, without
help, with no other aim than the one he sets himself, with no
other destiny than the one he forges for himself on this earth.
Never have I thought that I was the happy possessor of a
"talent"; my sole concern has been to save myself by work and
faith.   - J.P.Sartre 1905-1980*

Transformation by realizing that self-improvement is an "Inside
Job" is also a clear philosophy. Inside job implies the necessity for
change. Many of thee groups explain that the universe really does
not care about your "I", your [self], or your "Poor Me" Thinking.
Thus, this school of thought tends to believe that you and your
"track record" are direct result or the "sum total" of your actions
and experience. Thus, without action, the record can't change.
Authenticity is also a prime spotlight issue of these courses. Like
ancient Taoism, authenticity is most closely linked to your "natural
expression". Being, doing, and receiving is also a methodology that
is espoused. Being is mostly about expressing your ideals and
aspirations that you are naturally drawn to.   With this
transformation, people learn that conforming may not be authentic
if it is just to look good. Self suffering for attention can also be
inauthentic. Righteous and passionate causes can also be

inauthentic by helping avoid confronting or thinking over the position that you take on an issue. The other lessons are usually devoted to relationships and how to improve them. Getting past the EGO, "being right", and criticism toward a place of awareness, respect, love, and listening can always enhance relationships. Lastly, the "if and when" mentality can be extremely inauthentic because a person is always waiting for something to happen before taking action or achieving peace of mind.[viii]

"Life always gets harder towards the summit-the cold increases, responsibility increases." Friedrich Nietzsche 1844-1900

Spiritual and Success Exercises

1. **Visualize Your Day -** At night, review your day – hour by hour. Try to remember what you did from the time you woke up to the end of the day. See each event, each interaction, each relationship. After visualization, consider the things that you could have done better. With this precept of order, much like the spiritual exercises of Ben Franklin over 200 years ago, you may build your character as well as your imagination skills each day.

2. **Contemplative Prayer -** Prayer, breath-work, meditation, visualization, and recognition of health and peace can be taken point by point through the body using a quasi-chakra observance system. When doing the health exercises in this book, you also imagine a healing light going through each chakra region.

Exercise: Sit in a chair or lie down. Close your eyes. Take in air through your nose, hold it for seven seconds, and then let it out of your mouth slowly. Do this at least three times to enter a relaxed state. Clench your fists and extend your fingers as far as they will go a few times and put your hands in your lap. Now clear your mind and imagine a peaceful scene such as a mountain meadow with flowers or a calm lake. Now, begin with the top of your head or crown, or you can also begin with the base or lower body. Go through each of the seven sections in one direction. The first letters of the colors are ROY.G.BIV (red, orange, yellow, green, blue, indigo, violet) with red beginning with the lower body and the head/crown corresponding to the color violet.

Now, go through all seven colors one by one, imaging the color of each chakra and the corresponding section of the body. Imagine each color purifying and regenerating the body, one by one. Relax and purify each section of the body one by one. When you have finished the exercise from crown to lower or lower to higher, release any impure energy to the universe while taking a few breaths from the nose and blowing out from the mouth. Then, express a mental thanks to the Supreme for the healing energy. Then open your eyes.

1. Muladhara (Sanskrit: Mūlādhāra) Lower body - our connection to the earth and the physical plane – Survival and Operation – Color: Red

2. Swadhisthana (Sanskrit: Svādhisthāna) Reproductive gland region of the body – our creative and procreative urges and drives – Color: Orange

3. Manipura (Sanskrit: Manipūra) Stomach/navel - energy center for power and manifestation and desires (location: solar plexus) – Color: Yellow

4. Anahata (Sanskrit: Anāhata) Heart - energy center for love – Color: Green

5. Vishuddha (Sanskrit: Viśuddha) Throat - center for expression – Color: Blue

6. Ajna (Sanskrit: Ājñā) Eyebrow or forehead between brows - our psychic powers – Color: Indigo

7. Sahasrara (Sanskrit: Sahasrāra) Top of head and crown - connection with the Cosmic or the divine. – Color: Violet

3. **Breathing and Purification –** Try to learn the purification breath work. Breathe slowly into your nose and out from your mouth. Imagine negative energy leaving your body with each exhale and see yourself with each intake breath taking in life, love, pure energy, and healing elements.

4. **Sensory Perception** – Learn to feel each part of the body uniquely. Sit or lie down and close your eyes. Then, pick a part of your body. Sense it, feel it, imagine where it is. If a part of your body has aches, pains, or dis-ease, then use this exercise to send healing energy to that spot in a targeted way.

5. **Constructive Journaling** – Every month or every three to six months, sit down and write out things that you are proud of. Write 10 things that you have done to improve your life in recent months. List your best attributes. Write out 5-10 things that you enjoy doing or would like to try. List things that you can do to respect yourself. Even write out a few luxury to-dos where you can take action each year to treat yourself to a trip, family fun, to luxury, or to learning.

6. **COT: Cognitive Occupational Therapy** – Every few days or weeks, you must do things that are cognitive and that involve neuroplasticity exercises. Examples are: learning to recite a poem or prayer, working puzzles, crosswords, or even chores such as unloading the dishwasher, building a model, writing a story, telling a story, preparing and giving a presentation or related activities. The "mind-hand" or "mind-speech" activity is very stimulating and builds mental muscle.

7. **Vibration -** Your vibration can be at many levels. To say the least, you can enhance your mental vibration through various actions. Higher levels of mental and spiritual vibrations include Love, Gratitude, Praise, Faith, Feel Good Emotions, and more. Many practitioners work on a daily basis to enhance and bring their mental and spiritual vibration to a higher level. Practitioners do this so that

they may lead a more harmonious life, but also to attract people, events, and things of the same or higher vibration. The end result of healthy vibrations is the attraction of more constructive events, outcomes, and possibilities.

8. **Euphoric Modeling –** Recall a certain past event or image that brings feelings of joy, happiness, peace, love, or endearment. Have this MOMENT at your beck and call. Whenever you feel a pestering negative thought, seize upon the moment of peace and seek out solutions, forgiveness, and peace of mind.

9. **Cause and Effect** - For every thought, action, or inaction, there is a corresponding thought and event. Your heartfelt emotions when mixed with constructive thought and action carry more force than the average thought and action. Building a foundation is vital to this step. At first, we must change our mentality from one of lack to a consciousness and mind of possibility. Our minds and hearts evolve and begin to believe in opportunity and abundance. Instead of thinking why, we transcend to a spiritual position of why not. At this juncture, we begin to take action in accordance with our dreams. Each mental and physical action we take on a daily basis adds to the momentum of our spiritual force. Our spiritual force in conjunction with our harmonious and constructive thinking begins to manifest higher realities in our days to come.

10.   **Habits and Routines** – Develop healthier routines by seeking out activities that build your life and improve your circumstances. Learn to reward yourself for superior habits. Sit down with a trusted advisor and analyze your daily routines. Review your rituals, what you watch, how you exercise, how you think, where you go, who you associate with, what you do to respect yourself. Evaluate all of these things and then determine how to better treat yourself to a life of excellence, self-regard, transformation, and fewer distractions.

The Twelve-Fold Path of Prosperity ™

In this age of a fast-paced and high-tech world, people are, more and more, seeking a strategic path to: authentic health, inner peace, better careers, and success. Becoming a warrior at true peace with yourself is the first key to happiness. Bridging your actions to your spiritual mind and body is where success can naturally emerge. To manifest a greater destiny, a person must make an informed inventory of their assets and desires. Each of us must 1) Analyze the results of our recent track record 2) Make a diagnosis of what tactics are good or bad 3) Create a plan to improve our lives on mental, physical and spiritual levels 4) Implement the new strategic actions 5) Monitor the ongoing results 6) Take corrective measures from time to time. To implement a new plan, we must form a clear and definite mental image of the results that he or she wishes to have, to achieve, or see the ideal image of what he or she wants to become. The seeker must cultivate his or her new beliefs using a higher order of imagination so as to feel worthy of greater heights. Throughout these 12 steps below, we will discuss the twelve keys to joy, flow, excellence, peace, and abundance. The person who wants to have an abundant life and prosperity must accurately develop his or her purpose and learn to imagine living the life that he or she would want to live. A true seeker of prosperity will learn to see their presumed destinies with an earnest thanksgiving that his new reality is manifesting.

This is the methodology by which mental energy or mental impressions are transferred over to the universe, and the creative forces are set in motion like a tiny chain reaction of activity. Each of us must use proper attention and concentration intertwined with harmonious mind, faith, and gratitude that is all rooted in love.

Your higher consciousness will then begin working with you to allow greater attention, concentration, and natural expression on a higher level. Defining your purpose in life or aiming toward specific outcomes while letting them unfold in the best ways will be where the miracles appear. Moreover, allowing your talents, true place, and right career to expand will also be a powerful part of your journey. Ultimately, developing stronger: concentration, thoughts, speech, and a greater worldview to support your actions and goals will be the catalyst of newfound successes. Combining the awakened mind with action is where your results begin to appear and build momentum towards tremendous growth and expansion.

1. Constructive Motives with Attentiveness

The first principles of the path, attention and concentration, are described as a laser focusing of the mind, which is a state in which all cognitive faculties are unified and directed to a particular objective. This is not simply being aware of your environment, but being conscious of your thought energy. By thinking, an earnest desire is brought to you, and by acting, you bring the desire into reality. While staying focused with faith and purpose, imagine your desired objective with all your heart and with all your strength, and with all your concentration. Hold the vision of yourself with the highest and best result on the picture screen of your mind. Next, use your current abilities or position as a means of developing yourself and continuous improvement. Keeping a vision of your purpose or goal held with confident expectation and purpose will cause the universe to move toward you with the right possibilities for your growth. Further, your action, if performed in the light of the intention of harmony and concentration, will bring you continuous, creative opportunity. See the life that you want as if it is pure possibility and as part of your essence. See yourself in possession of the life and abilities that you so desire. Make use of them in your imagination as if they are your present reality. Meditate upon your purpose and vision until it is clear and distinct, and then take the mental attitude of ownership toward everything in that picture. Take possession of success in your mind, in the full belief that is truly yours. Hold to this vision and do not waiver in your belief that what you desire is yours in heart and mind. And remember to be thankful for blessings received and new inspiration "at all times," as you would when it has taken form. If we can thank the universe for what is imagined in the mind, we will have prosperity and peace, and we will become co-creators of everything that we earnestly want.

Remaining contemplative in action is also part of being in the moment. Your awareness is your "Life Force Consciousness." With focus and refinement of mind, your awake-ness will be natural and potent. You will see and sense new ideas and feel the power of intuition and knowingness. You will recognize when to act and how to act, and you will be in tune with the infinite.

2. Higher Purpose in the World

Everyone should engage in a career and occupation that he or she enjoys in a spiritual and productive way. All persons can follow their dreams and exercise their God-given talents in a way that naturally expresses their life force. Therefore, we should be able to feel proud of our work while being rewarded for what we have created and produced for others. This is the law of compensation and flow. A higher purpose involves win-win relationships in which everyone benefits. Our work can be for the good of all those involved, where everyone gets some kind of increase in their lives due to operating with higher purpose. Before becoming fearful of ambition, realize that poverty, misery, and sacrifice are not pleasing to anyone. Ambition is merely a desire to adapt, grow, and create. In contrast, pretending to be poor, charitable, or miserable to achieve attention is a losing proposition. Remember that extreme altruism is no better and no nobler than extreme selfishness, where both are forms of greed. Thus, we can and must believe in the possibility of growth, wealth, and prosperity. As such, we do not have to entertain the idea of scarcity or competition. To achieve abundance, we must create and innovate. We must become who we are supposed to be and there is no need to compete for the little scraps of food from the table when abundance is plentiful. You know people who work in a field of joy who prosper, and you can do this also. You do not have to take anything from anyone. You do not have to cheat, steal, or take advantage in negotiations. You can operate from a win-win perspective where all benefit from your contributions. You must become a creator, not a competitor, and you will get what you want, but in such a way that each person will have more because of your actions.

3. Specificity of Vision & Contemplation

Contemplation of your intentions is similar to planting the seed of your vision or purpose. If we are definite in our intentions and purpose, our dreams can unfold along the lines of our true path. Writing down our intentions is also magical, and has a superb effect, especially in clarifying our direction and goals to ourselves and upon our subconscious mind.   However, it is in our mindset that we cultivate what we really want. In order to coalesce our consciousness toward any direction, we must "focus relentlessly during all hours." And this means holding constant attention to your vision, with the intent to cause the transformation of our ideas into form. We can operate on a plane of mental harmony and good will, and we can flow constructively with life. It is better not to resist potentiality. We can allow life to unfold in conjunction with our constructive and faithful action. We can make the best of ourselves while in a state of peace and wellbeing. Our highest truth is harmony, bliss, health, and success.

4. Strategic Communication

Safeguard your communications both internally and externally. We should NOT speak of ourselves or our affairs unless with confidants who desire success for us. Never talk about life, career, or the economy as sad, or business conditions as terrible. Times may be hard but business is only bad for those who are operating with a scarcity consciousness.

Remember, you are a constructive creator, your ideas help people, your ideas do not take away from anyone, you can create what you want, and you are above fear. When others are having hard times and poor business, you will find your greatest opportunities. Right communication means the way you talk to others and to yourself. Train yourself to think and speak of life getting better and better with unlimited supply. Always speak in terms of forward movement; to do otherwise is to deny your faith.

5. Bold, Efficient Action

Every action that we take is either productive or ineffective. Each inefficient action is non-productive, and if you spend your life doing inefficient things, you will not enjoy peace or success. The more wasteful things that you do, the worse for you. On the other hand, if your every action is constructive, and if every act of your life is efficient, your whole life will be successful. The causation of failures is doing things in an inefficient manner without focus, and not doing enough things in an efficient manner. You will see that it is a self-evident proposition that if you avoid inefficient acts, and if you do a sufficient number of constructive acts each day, you will enjoy a richer and fuller life.

Every action that is backed by an earnest desire must be strong. Every act can be made strong by contemplating or knowing your purpose while you are doing it. If you also put all the power of love, faith, and gratitude in your action, it can further magnify your power and focus. Ultimately, we must create the means to capture, receive, and harvest the fruits that life offers to us so that we can use it for our development and also help mankind. While these steps force creation into motion, your desires may not appear according to your specific wants but rather manifest in a greater or more appropriate outcome at a later date. Never allow yourself to feel disappointed if this is the case. You can expect to have a certain thing at a certain time, but not get it at that time, and it will appear as a loss. But if you hold to your faith, you will find that the failure is only temporary. It may be a lesson to take a fresh path. If you do not receive the desired outcome, you may soon get something much better, and you will see that the apparent loss was really a great success.

6. Harmonious Mind

Mindfulness is the controlled and perfected faculty of cognition. It is the mental ability to see beyond what is apparent with clear consciousness.   To do this, you must acquire the ability to think the way you want to think. This is the first step towards achieving abundance. Thinking what you want to think is controlling your mental imagery and inner voice, which is enabling truth regardless of appearances. Every person has the natural and inherent power to think what he or she wants to think with practice. Seeing past what seems evident is possible if you are willing to train yourself and allow yourself to grow on a spiritual and metaphysical level. The more you can harmoniously focus your mind while imagining all of your goal's details, the better. This will bring the Supreme Force into accord with your highest good where the Universe must cooperate with you. Mental harmony also implies that we should be aware that others on this earth are here to help us and may offer assistance. We should be in tune with these opportunities that may come from many places in the form of other people seeking us out. Harmony is achieved and cultivated by keeping your mind clear of confusion, where it has room to allow flow and goodness to freely enter.

7. Effective Comprehension – Understanding

This means seeing, understanding, interpreting. and believing the highest truth. At our lowest level of existence, we see all things as misery and suffering. We can achieve a higher order of living if we can see life as a miracle and go beyond what the critical mind can see. Having the correct view provides peace of mind, the ability to act, the enhanced possibility of good fortune, and a sense of wellbeing. In the same vein, we manifest internally and externally the thoughts that we think about all day. So our views and how we focus our attention are extremely important. Thinking ideas of abundance, health, love, and so on, is a force much greater than any negative ideas. Sometimes, the correct interpretation of our next move is simply doing what is ahead of us, one thing at a time, with excellence, and doing things right the first time. For higher understanding, we develop a state of mind that is conducive to our desires. We direct positive thoughts, enthusiasm, belief, and persistence to be built on truth. Truth can be perceived in a constructive way or we can base our truth on lack or negativity. We all know that a bitter and negative attitude is not an effective way to live and can actually program persons for failure. As they say, *"Realists Expect Failure & Demand to Be Right."* Seeing constructive potentiality takes skill and practice. When exercising the principles of a comprehensive awareness, you will expand this skill over time.

8. Joyful Effort

Having a sense of flow with your work and endeavors can be seen as a reward from utilizing a combination of the principles of the 12-fold path. Nothing can be achieved without effort, which is in itself an act of will, whereas non-definite effort distracts the mind from its task, and confusion may be the consequence. Thus, you must really desire prosperity in your work life. This, in effect, can be compared to detached but focused activity, where you are flowing with the universe with non-resistance of mind.

The clearer and more definite you see yourself in flow and success, the stronger your effort will become, and the stronger your power, the easier it will be to hold your mental energy fixed upon the outcome of what you yearn for. Behind your earnest and specific vision must be the essence to realize and recognize it, to bring it into corporeal expression. Right efforts mixed with confident expectation or faith will become natural productivity animated with results. Behind this intention must be an invincible and unwavering belief that the reward is already yours and that you already have it in possession in your mind's eye. Thus, you need only to take ownership of it psychologically and accept it with an open mind to own it. Live in the new objective, mentally, until it takes form around you physically. No haste is required. However, we know energy is more effective with preparedness. Even the mighty Lincoln said that if he had eight hours to cut down a tree, he would spend six sharpening the axe. Thus, being ready in your mind, body, and Spirit can enable a seamless flow of action. In the mental realm, enter into full enjoyment of the things you want. "Whatsoever things ye ask for when ye pray, believe that ye receive them, and ye shall have them," said The Great Master.

9. **Open to Receive Inspiration**

Many people from around the world feel unworthy of abundance. Many do not value themselves, their abilities, their talents, or their work. It is very important to learn to feel worthy and deserving of good. You are a unique and spiritual being created by the universe with a celestial purpose. As a unique being in communion with the universal flow of ideas, you should become mentally open to receiving all good things in life. Further, people should be careful to allow the receipt of blessings into their lives from the Universe and from others. *Example*: Accepting a compliment from another person or having a method of being rewarded financially.

True and lasting Prosperity has a spiritual foundation that includes balance. Successful persons master excellence in body, mind, and spirit. When there is balance, ideas and energy flow from the universe to the person who is exercising this higher realm of existence. When we are at our best and acting as spiritually effective individuals, we actually have more ideas flowing to us from the "universal mind" or consciousness of the infinite.

Therefore, we can participate in our destiny and co-create our own reality. If you read the great spiritual minds of the Renaissance, you will quickly see that it is the right of the individual to have a direct experience with the Deity of your understanding through prayer, meditation, and getting back to the spiritual basics. Taking quiet time to meditate, pray or contemplate, may indeed create an untold mystical flow of inspiration to all who try.

10. Gratitude and Belief – The Vibration

Gratitude and Thankfulness lead to greater constructive expectation in our daily living. Positive expectation and confident expectation that is based in belief IS THE SUBSTANCE OF FAITH.

Recognize possibility, praise others, bless others, and bless and praise yourself. Blended with humility, your harmonious connection to universal spirit will allow a pipeline of grace to flow upon you. A thankful heart is highly conducive to faith, bliss, and living with joy. Realize that you are free to create abundance and that you are worthy of the gifts of the universe. With your higher belief, you free your mind's mental and spiritual power to focus on what you want. What you think about becomes expansive in your life. Your focus on the good and the great will bring these miracles into your world.

Faith and Belief are the deciding energy in many situations. All things created equal, the scientific probability of a coin toss result is 50 percent in its purest form. However, it only takes a grain of sand to tilt the balance of a scale in one direction. Thus, something as small as a mustard seed on one side of the balance can, in fact, lean the probability of prosperity in one direction versus another. In sum, the cosmic cards can begin to be dealt in your favor with the influence of intention and gratitude. In the end, happiness and gratitude are reasonable options that lead to the greater possibility of success and peace of mind.

11. Love Energy and Forgiveness

Love is the quality of thought and emotion that will propel us into a state of bliss and achievement.

Love all there is. Focus on the good, the great, the constructive, and the beauty of life. See the best in all there is. Look for the good that occurs in the world.

Meditate on the people who have been kind to you, the creation all around you, the good that happens every day, the inventions for the betterment of humanity, and the positive happenings around the world that occur each and every day. Learn to love all and love yourself, and love will be attracted to you. Love is a composite of many things including gratitude, harmlessness, peace, kindness, and compassion. Thinking love and giving love will liberate you into the fourth dimension of harmony. Think of how you have already been blessed, protected, and guided throughout your life. Yes, lessons have been learned, and further happiness, peace, and success may be yours if you stay on the path of quantum bliss.

Cultivating love and forgiveness can dispel otherwise discouraging thoughts. Great minds can look back on things they love or loved, and recapture that emotion. Empower yourself and your spiritual self with love, gratitude, kindness, harmonious thinking, harmless action, and serenity. Your dreams will be realized as long as you do not resist the gifts of abundance and remain aware of life's gifts.

Contemplate the concepts of St. Paul: Patience, Kindness, Understanding, Generosity, Sincerity, Humility, Gentleness ... Love never Fails.

12. **Wisdom - Having these qualities: Knowledge Perception**

Wisdom is said to be composed of the qualities of: experience, knowledge, and good judgment. Acting with wisdom is said to be the path of prosperity. Having money, good looks, or power is not necessary, but having wisdom is a requirement for health, happiness, and success. As they say, a man with money meets a man with experience, and the man with the money gets an experience, and the man with experience ends up with the money.

Having the power to picture potentiality and make healthy decisions and winning choices will create a life of prosperity and abundance. While wisdom is crucial, acting upon it is also the mother of the greatest successes in history.

* These concepts from *The 12-Fold Path* are inspired by the combined teachings of many great masters such as: Pythagoras, Marcus Aurelius, Schopenhauer, Hegel, Swedenborg, Emerson, Napoleon Hill, William Walker Atkinson, Charles Haanel, Genevieve Behrend, Epicurean Thought, Stoicism, Taoism, Confucianism, Thoreau, and W. Wattles. Everything is possible with desire, faith, love, harmonious action, and constructive thinking. Remember that these are important steps in our pursuit of excellence and peace. Take the best ideas from the list and use them to improve your life:

Twelve Meditations and Affirmations for Peace of Mind

- **Affirmations** -   Each Statement can be said silently or out loud. These meditations are designed to bring you closer to harmony with the universe, improve your self-esteem, and augment peace & abundance.

The first 12 meditations are a flowing but simple affirmation methodology to clear your mind an soul. Some people may want to go the most traditional route and read and meditate on one per day.

1st Meditation -. I surrender to the love of the Universe. I now am free to live, learn, love, laugh, and listen. I have changed and improved myself. I love and respect myself. I have stopped resisting the Universe and now cooperate with its power, and this has given me the victory of harmonious living. Today, I will live in harmlessness. Life will unfold for positively for me

2nd Meditation - I have serenity and peace. The universal power has granted me freedom and clarity. I am calm, relaxed, and cool. I am not in a hurry. My sense of well being keeps me in harmony with all.   The universe has restored me to wholeness and satisfaction. I have all that I need for today.   The Supreme Intelligence takes care of me. I am a child of God. God loves me. God is the Great Spirit that protects me.

3rd Meditation - Today, I serve the Great Spirit instead of my ego. I am connected with The Great Power. The great power gives me courage and wisdom. The great universal power is the force and source of my prosperity. Abundance is mine now. Everything I need will be provided by the abundance of the great power. I turn my daily thoughts over to my Higher Self. I give my financial, relationship, work, family, and other issues over to the care of the

Universe. I continue to do my part to be the best I can be.   I am free because I release all of my problems or challenges to the power greater than myself.

4th Meditation - I work to keep a clear and free conscious. I will continue to engage self analysis. I will identify the good things about myself. I will also find where I have done harm or been caused discomfort. I have worked to mend and clear up the past. I live a self respecting life today. I am proud of myself. I have values today that give me satisfaction because the values that I have are good for me. I take care of myself. I make healthy decisions. Thus, I am healthy in mind, spirit, and soul.

5th Meditation - I have discussed my past wrongs with another and with my Higher Self. I have been given great relief from working through this process of freeing my mind and forgiving myself and others. I have freed my heart and mind from the old resentments, jealously, hatred, envy, pride, greed, lust and so on. I have diffused the old negative thoughts by discussing issues with another in confidence. I have now made room for more good in my life. I am grateful for this release and this process. I am happy, enthusiastic, and energetic.

6th Meditation - I am willing to identify parts of my character that are not good for others and me. I am willing to work on improving my character and being a better person. Today, I am much better because I have lessened or eliminated some of these destructive behaviors. I am grateful that the Universal Force allows me to change for the better. My Higher Self has helped me change and improve many things. Today, I view myself as strong, vital, whole, complete, beautiful, and loving.

7th   Meditation - I remember who is in charge.   I am not the Supreme Master.   The Universe is the source of my happiness. I engage harmonious living today.   I am a loving and tolerant person. I am happy because I am comfortable with myself.   I take time today to be grateful for the things that I have. I have health. I have love. I care about others and myself.   I remember where I came from. I am willing to be good to myself and help others today. I am strong and happy because of all of the work I have done to get where I am right now.   I cooperate with the universal spirit

8th Meditation -   I live in harmony with others today. I love myself, and I radiate love because of this. I am willing to make amends to the people that I have harmed. . Today, my heart and mind are free because of my spiritual work. I feel so happy today because I have cleared a path to freedom. I am grateful that I have the tools and strategies to live a harmless and loving life. People respect and love me because I am respectful and loving. I have rebuilt many bridges, and I will create and improve relationships for the rest of my life.

9th   Meditation - I am willing to apologize and forgive sincerely if needed. I admit my wrongs in my heart, mind, and in person. The recipient of my atonement at some point will understand my actions. Today, I can correct a mistake affecting another and take action to free us both of this situation.

10th Meditation - If and when I act wrongly, I will try to clean up the mess right then. I can live in harmony and humility while being a strong and intelligent person.   I am stronger because I have dissolved a weakness. Today, I live in harmony. Today, I am at peace. I need not retaliate. My silence can be a skill. I can delay my reaction or retaliation. I do not need to be right all of the time.

I can be a listener instead of the talker. I have a plan, and the plan will make me a greater person and give me peace.

11th Meditation - I take time to meditate. I take time for prayer. Even if it is only for one minute before I go to sleep or upon awakening. Today, I serve the will of my Higher Power. I am connected to the source. I am now close to my Higher Power. This connection grants me strength, courage, serenity, health, love, and the ability to work hard. I can do all things through my higher power because my higher power protects and loves me.

12th Meditation - I am totally awake spiritually. I am new, and I have returned. I feel so blessed. I practice humility, gratitude, and love in my life. I try to live in harmony with all. My service to others has given me life and strength. I live a constructive and self-respecting lifestyle. I am responsible. Other people who need my help remind me of where I came from. I am grateful for these people. Today, I realize that I have received a spiritual revitalization, and I am thankful for it. I look back and identify all of the changes that I have made, and I realize the sum of the changes is the miracle of my life.

Results Will Prove You Right – Analyze, Diagnose and Clarify

We are herein focused on results and results ONLY. If the system works, then there is no refuting its POWER.

Half measures will avail you nothing. You must not be a wishful person but rather a focused person filled with belief. Rather than sitting around thinking about what you would do if you won the lottery, maybe there is another way. Maybe the people that are relatively wealthy and happy are doing something different to achieve these coveted results?

Would you like a change? Do you want improvement? Are you willing to train your mind to new successful habits and character?

If you are ready, then there is a science to success and a clear and concise path to wealth, health and prosperity.

All of us are using only a FRACTION of our abilities. Each one of us is a powerhouse of energy, consciousness, ideas and action.

From Pythagoras to Plato, from Spinoza to Hegel, and from Schopenhauer to Einstein, the great thinkers of all time imply the same thing. They claim that there are unseen cosmic forces that we can tap into that can energize and guide us to ideas, inventions, power and greatness.

Many of us want things but have we really been sincere? To achieve, we must be truly earnest about our goals. We must have that burning desire, which is something that you will go after and NEVER look back. This is a feeling of authentic PURPOSE where you will dedicate your whole heart to your betterment and becoming your best.

To make this big advancement, you must be willing to let go of your preconceptions. Give up your old ways and become open to a new path, new power and new abundance. What would you do if you could not fail? Truly ask yourself and petition your subconscious for inspiration and guidance. Ask for ideas, ask for help and ask for some sign that will lead you to new heights.

If you are willing to make this quantum leap, get out of your comfort zone and then learn a guaranteed method to riches and success if you are willing to put it to use with PERSISTENCE.

Unlimited Power is Yours

You have within you the power to connect to the universal force. This force is the creative and animating energy that permeates the universe. Like gravity or electricity, the Force is not seen, but exists as the all-pervading framework for which every law hinges upon. This interstellar force is also known as God or "The Life Force". This unlimited power is everywhere as creation is constant. New ideas, new art & music, new planets, new galaxies, new species, new worlds are continuously manifesting at this very moment.

That part of your mind that can be in-tune with this force is referred to by the great teachers of metaphysics as the subjective mind or higher consciousness.   Directed thought-energy can be focused where the individual may act as a creative force within the universal framework.   This supernatural power is willing to serve you and grant you anything that you earnestly and sincerely desire with focus, action, heartfelt gratitude and emotion. If Faith is the substance of things hoped for, then that very Substance can also be qualified as the energy of our attention and thoughts.   Belief and faith are the same in that they mean that we accept what is unseen. Energy is consciousness, and thus, "thought awareness" is energy. All things created equally in perfect balance, the energy of faith, attention, and mind can tilt the cosmic balance of life, happiness, and success in our favor.   This is why spiritual-metaphysics is so important because the participant who engages mental-cooperation with universal law attains the ability to optimize: body, mind and spirit. The galactic framework of forces that we seek to cooperate with is what many call: "the Spirit of the Universe" and "the spirit within you". All of us go through life with a steady stream of ideas, thoughts, and desires. Tapping into that greater, infinite-self expands our intuitive abilities to best use our priceless inspiration. Thus, becoming aware that we may operate at a higher order of being is where achievement truly begins, and then, we become willing to take the actions that provide results. Co-operation with the "force of the universe" and the framework of the metaphysical laws that affect mankind is the path to maximize our existence, contributions, and consciousness.   Learning to use the mind and concentrate on our desires is where self actualization begins. Even the great Marconi was referred to the insane-asylum by government officials for suggesting that information and thoughts can be sent over the airwaves.   However, today all of us know that we can tune into any given channel and send messages millions of miles. Harnessing the power of prayer, meditation and contemplation is where inspiration and well-being is cultivated. With this power of mental focus and cooperation with the universal law, we become masters of our destiny.

The Master Key List – The Plan

Begin your new life today. Write out 5, 10 or even 50 things that you want to do to improve your life and circumstances. Don't be shy! Write the amazing and exciting things you will achieve about money, travel, relationships, health or whatever. Do it and do it today. As the great poet von Goethe once implied, Begin it TODAY and there is MAGIC and POWER in it.

Write out your Master Key List and put it in your pocket. Think about it for a day. Then pick the 3 most important things you can do to change your life for the better and begin immediately to commit to those 3 goals.

Every day, when you are in your Alpha Relaxed State, you can read the list to yourself. Read it at night and upon awakening. Think about the completed successes. Think about the ESSENCE of your purpose and how you can help yourself, your family and others by attaining your dreams.

As part of your continual growth, you can enhance, add, expand and remove things from your Master Key List.

A Mental Agreement for Specific Success

Your plans and mental blueprint should be very specific. For example, you can write out on a piece of paper a personal commitment to yourself:

> *I, Joe Kahn, Jr., will have a million dollar business 5 years from today. I will sell super creative solutions. I will provide the best service and value to my customers. My products and services will have outstanding benefits for everyone. I will do my best, work hard and remain persistent. I will not falter. Everybody will be happy to pay me handsomely for my services because they will feel great benefits from what I/we provide. I will gladly accept compensation and I will do what is needed to capture and utilize the funds. Sincerely, Joe K, August 2021*

Exercise: If we invoke the INNER POWER/SELF and EARNESTLY ask for [help, harmony and cooperation] , we are drawing closer to the Source. If we can meet the Source halfway, stay tuned into the POWER, and cooperate with the Life Force, our advancement will be speedy.

Exercise: Take some deep breaths ... You mental vibration is important. Can you take time to energize the way you feel about your goal? ... Think about a result that you want. Feel the joy of seeing it. Sense it. Emotionalize it. See your desired result in your mind's eye. Visualize it. Think As If it is YOURS. Think grateful thoughts for the imagined result or something better being manifested in your life. Send the wonderful loving thoughts into the world with heartfelt gratitude and knowing that the universe will bless you on your journey.

Definiteness of Purpose - Knowing what you want and dedicating yourself to it.

Be definite about your desires. On your list:

1. Specify what the desire is. Examples: to weigh the same amount as you did when you graduated from high school, run a marathon, get a promotion, or obtain a better home.

2. Identify exactly what you will do to achieve it.

3. Specify precisely when you will achieve it.

4. Determine what it will feel like to have it and what it will look like.

5. Imagine how you will use your success and envision what emotions you will have when you attain or use your desired outcome.

6. Take some concrete action to move toward your success each and every day.

If the desire is money, then specify the amount, what you will give in exchange for the money and how you will use or invest the money.

While you are building yourself up, associate with those who know about success. Ask encouraging people who know about what you want for help. Many will be happy to give you advice. Model yourself after the best and focus on the best as your belief system will certainly change for the better. Continue to use praise and appreciation in your life as this act of blessing all people and things expands your goodness and brings prosperity and appreciation to you.

When you accomplish any little thing toward your happiness, recognize the goodness of the universe. Be grateful for every small achievement and bless each and every good event that comes your way. Gratitude dispels doubt, keeps you connected, and prevents dissatisfaction. Continue to fix your attention on health, love, success, and good fortune. Your faith will be renewed.

Sincere and heartfelt thankfulness will create a newfound faith in your abilities and allow you to be connected to the great POWER within you.

Initiate Action - Using The Secret Methodology - Tips To Ensure Success.

1. When you want something badly, be sure to allow the universe to bestow upon you the thing you want or something better. Do NOT limit the universe with your desires as the supernatural power may want to give you even more than you seek in new and untold ways.

2. Pray and meditate only for good to happen to yourself and others and avoid negative thoughts or feelings for others or over any situation.

3. See the benefits and purpose of your desire and understand how your desire can help you, all involved, and even assist greater humanity.

4. Seize control of your Charisma and learn to direct and master your Personal Magnetism.

5. Focus on being creative and not just competitive. You can win with your goals and desires by creating new opportunities for yourself and all people.

6. Try to maintain harmlessness in your actions, speech and thinking.

7. Maintain personal responsibility for your actions and take care of your spiritual condition.

8. Give without the expectation of receiving and donate your time and talent to organizations that divinely inspire you and lift up your consciousness.

9. Give your attention to pressing needs first and then when you are stronger as a person, you can go for bigger and bigger goals.

10. Learn all you can to make yourself ready and capable to achieve any of your stated desires. But remember to take action toward your goals NOW. Taking action can be reading a book, taking a course, calling somebody for an appointment or applying for a position.

11. Keep your consciousness and mental attitude clear and efficient. If you have done harm to others, try to make it right and continuously maintain your wellbeing by maximizing the excellence of your character by practicing attunement and atonement.

12. Make a decision. Without commitment and making something important, the ideal will only be a hopeful wish. Your job is to go to the next level and make your move to achieve what you want with all your heart and desire.

13. Affirm your destiny. Speak it aloud to yourself every day. Say your positive affirmations and prayers out loud in the present tense with feeling and emotion. Speak constructively and learn to speak in an optimistic and confident way.

Remember, one of the greatest abilities of mankind is to give love. We live for the advancement of body, mind and soul and there is no reason to limit our capacities. Many ignorant people see wealth as greed. Ironically, poverty can and will frustrate your relationships with the spirit, other people and those you love. Accordingly, giving is one of the highest forms of love. Give yourself everything you need to become an asset to your community and to the world where one day you may give back as much as you can in great measure.

The Steps to Success – Moving Toward Your Destiny

1. Remember that growth, prosperity and the ability to innovate, create and adapt is your birthright. You are born to be prosperous and excellent.
2. Desire is a power seeking expression. You cannot desire what is not potentially within you; and therefore, you can be what you want to be.
3. Desire is the result of feeling, and the feeling that results from a burning desire is a supernatural faculty seeking and demanding greater expression.
4. Use your free time to hone your skills, improve your knowledge and prepare for your dreams and goals. Do not wait for the perfect opportunity to be all that you want to be. Become all that you can be today, and when an opportunity to be more is offered to you, be ready to take it.
5. Use your place or present business and environment as the means to get a better one. Spend nights and weekends cultivating your abilities and preparing for greater things and the fulfillment of your goals.
6. Everything that touches your life is an opportunity if you discover its proper use. Be aware of each circumstance and study them all for they are your opportunities. Most men fail by hoping for some particular kind of luck, instead of being ready to seize opportunities.
7. Steadily hold the picture of all that you want to attain in person, property and environment. Form a clear conception of it. Then understand that in so far as your desires are not contrary to Eternal Justice, it is absolutely certain that you can be what you want to be. Dwell upon your goal and ideal until it is clear and definite to you and hold it until it arouses intense desire.
8. Your vision of the right idea, if held with faith and purpose, will cause the Supreme Intelligence to move the right opportunity toward you. Then your action, if performed with effectiveness and efficiency, will cause you to move toward the success.

9. Pray with unfaltering grateful faith to the Supreme Intelligence that your desires shall come to you and be thankful in every prayer, petition or affirmation. Express thanksgiving with a heart full of gratitude that your desires are coming to you.

10.   Think about this ideal picture until you are always conscious of it and become in conscious possession of it with positive emotion. Presume it is yours mentally.

11.   Desire for everybody what you want for yourself. Be sure to take nothing from anybody without giving a full equivalent in life and value; the more you give, the better for you.

12.   Use each day to the fullest and do each act efficiently and effectively without haste. You must put the expanding thought into everything you do and communicate excellence to all whom you deal with.

13.   Know that others from around the world desire to help you now that you are on the supernatural path. You are to cooperate and be willing to receive this mutually beneficial exchange and assistance from those who are sent to you.

14.   The basic element of success is therefore to hold the thought and the mental attitude of advancement and to be excellent in all that you do.

15.   Strive to maintain a Consciousness of your being at one with the Spiritual Power of the Universe. Know that you are connected to the Creative Power and begin now to co-create your destiny. Utilize these steps in all of your affairs.

You are chosen, naturally unique, knowing

What ever your race, believe that it is good and great. Whatever your education, believe that you can be better as more knowledge and understanding of the laws of life are needed. Regardless of your appearances, you can look better, improve yourself, be healthy, and enhance your image in your unique way. It does not matter what religion or philosophy you adhere to, your spiritual knowledge and awareness can be cultivated to a new dimension where peace of mind is yours. You are a Genius. You have been chosen to do great things and live a significant life. You have talent from the universe. You must allow your assets and skills to be honed and sharpened. Do not die with your vision and talents unused. You are special, and you can be whatever you want within your sphere of availability and grow accordingly toward your destiny. There is nothing wrong with being confident in who you are. Only good can come from growth. Sometimes change is difficult, but the re-invention or rebirth of your true self is available NOW

Quotes and Maxims

- ~ St. Francis ~ Birth Name/born Giovanni di Pietro di Bernardone - "Lord, make me an instrument of Your peace. where there is hatred, let me sow love; where there is injury, pardon; where there is doubt, faith; where there is darkness, light; and where there is sadness, joy." St. Francis of Assisi"

- ~ William James ~ "The potentialities of development in human souls are unfathomable. So many who seemed irretrievably hardened have in point of fact been softened, converted, regenerated, in ways that amazed the subjects even more than they surprised the spectators." William James

- Catherine Ponder ~ "Cleansing or purification is the first step in prosperity. Without releasing mentally, emotionally, and in our visible world, there can be no permanent, satisfying prosperity... Along with cleaning out the closets, clean up and clean out your life. The skeletons in the closet have got to go, if you wish to be truly prospered."

- ~ Nelson Mandela ~ "I am fundamentally an optimist. Whether that comes from nature or nurture, I cannot say. Part of being optimistic is keeping one's head pointed towards the sun, one's feet moving forward. There were many dark moments when my faith in humanity was sorely tested, but I would not and could not give myself up to despair."

- Warren Buffet ~ "We intend to continue our practice of working only with people whom we like and admire. This policy not only maximizes our chances for good results, it also ensures us an extraordinarily good time. On the other hand, working with people who cause your stomach to churn seems much like marrying for money—probably a bad idea under any circumstances, but absolute madness if you are rich."

- Henry Ford ~ "Good will is one of the few really important assets of life. A determined man can win almost anything that he goes after, but unless, in his getting, he gains good will he has not profited much."

- ~ Shunryu Suzuki ~ "If your mind is empty, it is always ready for anything; it is open to everything. In the beginner's mind there are many possibilities; in the expert's mind there are few."

- Felix Dennis ~ "The bottom line is that if I did it, you can do it. I went from being a pauper—a hippy dropout on the dole, living in a crummy room without the proverbial pot to piss in, without even the money to pay the rent, without a clue as to what to do next—to being rich. And I am certainly no business genius, as my rivals will happily and swiftly confirm."

- ~ Teresa of Avila ~ Born, Teresa de Cepeda y Ahumada "As I see it, we shall never succeed in knowing ourselves unless we seek to know God: let us think of His greatness and then come back to our own baseness; by looking at His purity we shall see our foulness; by meditating upon His humility, we shall see how far we are from being humble."

- Orison Swett Marden ~ "Don't wait for extraordinary opportunities. Seize common occasions and make them great."

- John Paul Getty ~ "To be truly rich, regardless of his fortune or lack of it, a man must live by his own values. If those values are not personally meaningful, then no amount of money gained can hide the emptiness of life without them."

- Peter Lynch ~ "Twenty years in this business convinces me that any normal person using the customary three percent of the brain can pick stocks just as well, if not better, than the average Wall Street expert."

- Richard Branson ~ ""I may be a businessman, in that I set up and run companies for profit, but, when I try to plan ahead and dream up new products and new companies, I'm an idealist."

- Sanaya Roman & Duane Packer ~ "Money is energy, and energy exists in all realms. The spiritual laws of money are universal energy laws that create abundance: the principles of ebb and flow, unlimited thinking, giving and receiving, appreciation, honoring your worth, clear agreements, magnetism, and more."

- Dr. Napoleon Hill ~ "No one has ever been known to achieve permanent success without doing more than he was paid for."

- Guy Kawasaki ~ "BE SPECIFIC. The more precisely you can describe your customer, the better. Many entrepreneurs are afraid of being 'niched' to death and then not achieving ubiquity. However, most successful companies started off targeting specific markets and grew (often unexpectedly) to great size by addressing other segments. Few started off with grandiose goals and achieved them."

- Marsha Sinetar ~ "The reason that this book's title contains the phrase, 'The Money Will Follow', is precisely because we must do the work first, invest of ourselves first, seed faithfully in the small, steady, incremental ways of our chosen work first, and then—as a harvest of abundant crops naturally follows the seeding, watering and constant caring process of seeds—the fruits of our efforts result."

- Adam Smith ~ The Wealth of Nations ~ "It is not from the benevolence of the butcher, the brewer or the baker that we expect our dinner, but from their regard to their own interest. We address ourselves, not to their humanity, but to their self-love, and never talk to them of our own necessities, but of their advantages. Nobody but a beggar chooses to depend chiefly upon the benevolence of his fellow-citizens."

- Prof. Wallace Wattles ~ "Riches secured on the competitive plane are never satisfactory and permanent; they are yours today, and another's tomorrow. Remember, if you are to become rich in a scientific and certain way, you must rise entirely out of the competitive thought. You must never think for a moment that the supply is limited."

- Brian Tracy ~ "The way for you to be happy and successful, to get more of the things you really want in life, is to get the combinations to the locks. Instead of spinning the dials of life hoping for a lucky break, as if you were playing a slot machine, you must instead study and emulate those who have already done what you want to do and achieved the results you want to achieve."

An Incomplete Recipe for a Higher Confidence

Please analyze each of these concepts as all are part of a higher order of living and knowingness.   As Carl Jung once said when asked about his faith, "I don't need to believe, I know"

1. Connectedness to the Universe
2. Gratitude
3. Acceptance of Goodness or Lack of Goodness
4. Attitude of Belief
5. Humility, Openness, and Personal-Power over Ego
6. Peace of Mind/Calm
7. Love and Harmlessness
8. Wholeness
9. Self Respect and Self Regard
10. Healthy Expectation of the Best
11. Knowingness and Mindfulness beyond Wishing and Hope.
12. Confidence in Doing What Works.
13. Being Contemplative in Action
14. A Higher Awareness
15. An Working Perceptive of the Substance of Things Unseen.
16. A Harmonious Relationship with God as the Life Force of All.
17. A deep understanding of the beneficence of the Universe and it's wondrous, imperfect and impersonal laws which govern our lives. A humble and confident comprehension that all is right with your world.

The Simple Prayer for Peace – By Sgr. G S Mentz -   JD MBA

Lord, Let us be a Beacon of Light and Harmony. May we serve you to maximize the joy, health, abundance, and aliveness in and of our world.

- Where there is Struggle, may there be Freedom
- Where there is Hope, may there be Success
- Where there is Dis-Ease, may there be Wholeness and Healing.
- Where there is Peace, may there be Prosperity, Order, and Tranquility.
- Where there is Change, may there be Innovation.
- Where there is Love, may there be Respect, Honor and Civility.
- Where there is Mindfulness, may there be Illumination and Awakening.
- Where there is Consciousness, may there be Spirituality and Serenity.
- Where there is Confusion, may there be Knowingness and Belief.
- Where there is Wanting, may there by Actualization.
- Where there is Victimhood, may there be Victory.
- Where there is Atonement, may there be Attunement
- Where there is Decision, may there be ACTION and Commitment.
- Where there is Justice, may there be Inner-Peace.
- Where there is Poverty, may there be a Righteous Labor of Love.
- Where there is the Past, may we contribute to the NOW.
- Where there is Uncertainty, may there be Authentic Faith.
- Where there is Meditation, may there by Clarity.
- Where there is Intelligence, may there be Pure Awareness.
- Where there is Pain, may there be Growth.
- Where there is Emptiness, may we be Filled with Joy and Abundance.
- Where there is Unity, may there be Serenity.

Summary of Ideas – A Parabolic Workbook to Success

Where there is Action, may we engage in Deeds that Stimulate Positive Outcomes.   O' Great Master, let us seek to empathize rather than console, to comprehend rather than understand, to love rather than be loved. While it is in earnestly giving that one receives, it is by forgiving that we own our freedom, and it is in illumination that one finds. For it is in transformation that one transcends, and it is in rebirth that one is raised to eternal bliss.

When we are Contemplative in Action, We can Express our Destiny, and We will never Be Defeated if we have Elevated our Spirit and Mastered our Consciousness.

Supernatural Workbook

The keys to your Destiny

1. The quality of your dominant thoughts is the causative and chief creative factor that produces success in all cases.
2. Cultivating the ability to withdraw attention from what is not useful in our life, is a great power.
3. Use your thought and mind to build worth and value into your life. Worth and character is built though abilities, performance, skills, mental perception, and results.
4. We must seek the experiences we want in our lives.
5. We must learn what those experiences we seek "would be like" so that we can sense and feel their manifestation in our minds eye.

6. We can maximize our imaginative abilities be practicing the art of seeing the future desired results in our minds eye.

7. We must remove the thoughts that don't serve us. Put recurring negative thoughts into a box, fasten it, and burn the box in your imagination, and send box or smoke away and release it permanently.

8. Decide that we will strive to avoid the same mistakes of the past. Past mistakes are sometimes priceless as we know how to navigate the obstacles when we try again.

9. What influences to we want in our life. News, Views, Friends, etc. What type of learning do you want? What type of exercise or strengthening activities do you want?

10.   What kinds of joys, peace and thoughts do you want to have?

Workbook Exercises:

Exercise – We Must Act "As If" in Mind and Action

1. Write things out that you want to be/do/have
2. Imagine these ideas being imprinted in & on your picture screen of subconscious mind.
3. Picture your fulfilled desires in your deeper mind as a fact and memory.
4. Feel the joy and aliveness of attainment of all you seek.
5. Repeat several days a week. Carry the list on paper with you.
6. Focus on your chief aims & primary intentions which will cause mind to disclose ideas & pathways for your success.
7. Act as if the life you seek is yours now. Be that person
8. Imagine a bright golden circle of protection and projection that radiates around you and protects your home and family. This golden circle of protection projects your successful energy of your future life.

Write out a few things that you want to have in your life:

1)____

2) ____

3) ____

4) ____

5) ____

Create present Tense Affirmations for All parts of Your Consciousness

1. Affirmations are speaking to your own consciousness either mentally or out loud. You can write affirmations out and read them to yourself or memorize them and say them to yourself.
2. You can handcraft Affirmations for yourself.
3. Write Affirmations out where you imagine the qualities of value that you want to have.
4. Imagine having all of these attributes such as strength, confidence, memory, confidence, poise, importance, value/worth, faith, skill, loving nature, academic abilities and more.
5. Imagine all of the great attributes surrounding you like an aura and radiating from your body and mind all the time.
6. Affirmations can be done by applying an affirmation to specific parts of your mindset.
7. When you instill yourself with affirmations, qualities, and a mindset of success, people begin to sense your energy.
8. Example: My health is excellent and every cell in my body is renewed each day, my mind and memory are excellent.

Write out a few Affirmations here:

1)____

2) ____

3) ____

4) ____

5) ____

Here are examples of affirmations directed at different parts of the SELF.

- I AM wealthy healthy and happy
- My soul and spirit are happy healthy and wealthy
- My deeper consciousness accepts that I am healthy and wealthy and happy
- My mind and memory are powerful and my mind remembers all necessary information.
- My heart, lungs, and organs are strong, vibrant and potent.
- From my head to my toes, my body and energy is strong, young, and full of endurance.
- My skin, aura, and body is healthy, vibrant, and strong.
- My perception and mental abilities are powerful and responsive.
- My mental, physical and spiritual health is wonderful and every cell of my body is renewed and energized every day.

Ask Yourself the Right Questions so that you can Activate Your Deeper Abilities

If we have not achieved success, many times we are not receiving what we seek because we have not looked at the right questions. We must ask ourselves the correct questions to allow the mind and memory and soul to absorb, comprehend, sense & feel the questions while working on the answers, and solutions to your challenges and your desires.

1. What would I like to have?
2. What would I like to be?
3. What would I like to do?
4. Where would like to go?
5. What would I like to create?
6. What do I want to look like.

If you don't have answers to these questions, you may just need more specificity in your life. We need to cultivate and develop priorities and options so that you may better be aligned with your destiny.

Write out jobs or things or successes that you would like to achieve/obtain.

1) ____

2) ____

3) ____

4) ____

5) ____

Find Out What Needs to Go!

1. Make a list of things that are not necessary in your life
2. Begin to "let go of" or avoid these unnecessary things or get rid of the habits, people, places or things that hold you back.
3. Find other healthy habits to replace what you have "let go of".
4. The ability to unravel conscious snags gives great power. Itemizing and discovering the obstacles that hinder you is important
5. Once itemized, then you can begin to create the intent to remove non-productive behavior and relationships.
6. Deep thinking about getting rid of dead weight and bad habits is a great start. This technically cultivates intent.
7. Mental obstacles are often great barriers to success, but many of them can be removed or even transformed.
8. Learning how to remove mental obstacles and eliminating deeper consciousness obstacles can give great power

Write out great habits that you can engage to replace old habits.

1) ____

2) ____

3) ____

4) ____

5) ____

Authenticity – Be True to Yourself

Being authentic about who you are & what you do gives you great enthusiasm and great creative ability

1. We don't have to be who our parents were. You need not have their job, profession, attitude, or life consequences.
2. You don't need to be what your brothers and sisters are in life. Whether they are doctors, teachers, or other, you don't need to be like them or compete with them.
3. You can break the Chain and become who you were meant to be. If bad things happened to you as a young person during your upbringing, you need not continue that way of thinking or acting of others in your family.
4. Write out who you think you should be by describing your future self, and describe those amazing characteristics that you seek. Imagine yourself being that what you seek "in the NOW".

Write out traits of our most authentic self.

1)____

2) ____

3) ____

4) ____

5) ____

The Stimulus – The Causation of Success

Motivation and Stimuli - We all know that every person has unique stimuli which motivates them to go great lengths to obtain what they seek. Therefore energy always follows your focus but sometimes to create focus we need some sort of stimuli. To create stimuli, investigate the various powers of your primary motivational desires.

<u>Try to APPEAL to your primary motivations</u>

1. Appeal to the power survival
2. Appeal to the power of passion
3. Appeal to the power of love
4. Appeals of the power of prestige
5. Appeal to the power of Hunger and creativity

If we can appeal to our greater desires, our dreams may outweigh the other distractions and habits that have been holding us back.

Write out what stimulates your desire to improve your life?

1)____

2) ____

3) ____

4) ____

5) ____

Serendipity and Synchronicity

Learn to act upon fate – Serendipity is the connecting principle that links mind to matter.

1. Learn to be still and open your heart and mind to the flow of ideas and inspiration from the universe.
2. Write down your great ideas.
3. Write down the tasks that are required to make these great ideas a reality.
4. Learn to be able to notice patterns in your life. Try to perceive the signs or symbols that enhance or confirm your opinions.
5. Learn to use inspiration. Learn to call that person or e-mail at person. When the thought to ask for help or insight comes to you, send that message out into the person. As long as the message does no harm, seeking to expand your life and relationships is good. Inspiration to connect to others works in mysterious ways.

Write out some ideas and patterns that you have had lately? This may be the universe guiding you to something.

1)____

2) ____

3) ____

4) ____

5) ____

The Spirit of The Universe

Why is The Spirit of the Universe important? God is the framework and the energy that binds the universe together. Learning to act in concert with the power of the universe gives us a great advantages and powers.

1. With awareness and focus, we can pay attention to our experiences.
2. We must learn to act and live towards the realization of our vision & learn how to use our willingness "as a power".
3. We must have resilience to be able to navigate challenges.
4. We must have alignment and make sure that our work is not going against our dreams. Do the results you are seeking look like a good-ethical and spiritual fit for you?.
5. Intentions are important. With empowering our intentions, we must maintain certain thinking and maintain certain actions which create a stimuli and catalysts to create what we seek.

Self Empowerment – For Work and Creativity

1. Make lists of your personality and character assets.
2. What products and services to you like the most and believe in?
3. It may be best to take a job with a company that has products and services we believe in.
4. Or start a company that creates products and services that you believe in strongly.
5. What is your purpose? An example of a purpose is "helping others have a better life in the areas of wealth health and happiness.
6. What are your core values?
7. We should be able to work and create in areas that do not conflict with our values

Satisfaction List - Do something that you want to do. Do you like to ?

a) Travel
b) Teach
c) Play music or listen to music
d) Create web sites are pictures
e) Write stories or essays
f) Speaking or acting

What can you do in these areas to enjoy life and make money

If you need education licenses; then, do the research and engage the learning that you need to master your destiny.

Write out some things you want to do, see, or new skill or new hobby.

1)____

2) ____

3) ____

4) ____

5) ____

Take Ownership:

Take ownership of Your Destiny which includes your:

1. Life
2. Work
3. Dream
4. Speech
5. Thought
6. Body
7. Mind
8. Soul

Write out a list of 5 things & you will take ownership of.

1)____

2) ____

3) ____

4) ____

5) ____

Learn as much as you can about

1. Yourself
2. Dreams
3. Goals
4. Job
5. School
6. Business
7. Or Do research on nights and weekends.
8. How you fit into the workforce.

Here's a list of the 12 Secret Powers of Achievement

1.   **Desire** – What do you truly and earnestly want to be, do and have.

2.   **Curiosity and Fascination** – What fascinates you? Something that you are passionate about will be both enjoyable and fun while expanding your life.

3.   **Love and Self Respect** – What are you doing to better yourself each day to make you feel good about who you are.

4.   **Wisdom and Knowledge** – What knowledge or skills do you need to maximize your future toward your destiny.

5.   **Inspiration and Intention** – Have you learned to tap into your creative mind? Sit still, and allow thoughts, ideas and solutions to come to you. It takes practice, but the mind is the great creator.

6.   **Analyze** – You must cultivate the awareness and mindset to look at and analyze challenges accurately.

7.   **Planning**- You must create plans or other people will make a plan for you. Planning involves making lists, itemizing tasks, and embedding ideas and goals into your mindset.

8.   **Patience and Persistence** – Are you willing to do what must be done each day to achieve your goals.

9.   **Action and Boldness** – Are you willing to begin and do each day what needs to be done. Each task is a step in the direction toward completion of a goal or group of goals.

10.   **Imagination and Vision** – Can you imagine and see your desired results for each goal you seek with specificity. Space, Size, Color, Sound, Feelings, Emotions, and Visual comprehension of what the completed success looks like?

11.   **Faith and Belief** – Faith is the substance of things unseen. It is belief and energy all wrapped into one unseen power. If you can maintain, focus, and utilize this energy, it will tip the scale of every undertaking in your favor.

12.   **Continuous Improvement and Momentum** – Are you willing to take time each year to better your character, skills, faith, and philosophical life.

You can do it. The 21st Century Effeciencies

With the type of technology that we have today with the ability to use computers and the Internet, we have 10 to 100 times greater research power than we did 20 or 30 years ago. You can take free courses online we can read books online for free, you can have books read to you online. You can search for jobs anywhere in the world with the stroke of a few keys.

What is your personality type. Overall you need to figure out whether you want to work for self a small company or large corporation in big organizational chart.

Most people generally speaking have worked for the government or a major corporation or small businesses for a few years before they set out on their own.

By getting work experience, they have learned key skills at these companies discovering how to deal of customers or repair things, learning about products and services.

If we work in a place that interests you, we can learn very much in just six months or in a matter of 2 to 3 years, we can learn a whole lot about how a company works.

Careers are 100% easier to research today. My father who was a Judge and brilliant scholar spent years researching a book that you could assemble and write in a week today. Another friend of my spent several thousand hours on genealogy research of which he could complete in as little as a week today

Thus, the world is vibrant and full of technology to help you.

Laws of Mastery

1. **Laws of Sowing** – Carefully picking the seeds you plant in your consciousness and sub consciousness. Careful sowing will allow the reaping of what you seek rather than weeds and failing crops.

2. **Consequences and Reaping – Receiving –** Receiving is a lost art to many. You must be ready and willing to accept the gift of good fortune with an open hand instead of a closed fist.. Further, you must be able to accept good fortune also by having the correct receptacle for receiving such good will such as bank accounts, value to exchange, services to provide, and so forth.

3. **Laws of Becoming** – You must learn to become that which you seek. If you want to be a successful Wall Street executive, you must become that person in character, skills, and habits.

4. **Law of Adapting and Lessons** – There is a seed of success in every opportunity. Even if you fail, you may later overcome the obstacle though new found knowledge, and lessons learned.

5. **Law of Character** – The law of character is simple but complex. Your character IS based on your thinking, actions and inactions. Learning to control these powers is true mastery.

6. **Law of Imagination, Focus and Imprinting** – Imagination is a skill that is developed. People who can visualize what they want and how they are able to get to it are masters of multi-dimensional chess in their minds.

7. **Law of Flow and Circulation** – There is a Yin and Yang to giving and receiving. We must not suffocate the flow of life force. Money is even a form of energy, and when we bless what we spend and thus expanding our energy flow. We give to people and organizations who either need it or divinely inspire us.

8. **Law of Alchemy and Transmuting** – Like a snake that molts its skin each year, we are constantly changing, growing and transforming. It is possible for us to let go of the old skin and morph into new and higher versions of ourselves. We must be willing to let go of the old and move to the new.

9. **Law of Supply and Ideas** – Substitutes – With every idea is a form of new supply. Some great business successes and authors only began with a single idea. Galaxies and stars seem to be created every year from nothingness. With everything that becomes scarce, something else seems to be created as a substitute. Always remember that creativity is the true raw material of our existence.

10. **The Law of Praxis** – 30 years ago, I never thought that basketball players or tennis players could be much greater than: Byrd, Magic, Borg or McEnroe; however, the field of human performance and praxis/practice seems to keep

expanding. If you look at the stats for NBA 3pt shooters for today compared to those of 20 years ago, the changes are significant and stunning. They say that many players today practice 2,000 shots a week. Thus, practices really does make perfect.

The Framework of Wealth – The Steps to Success

1. As beings that desire increasing life, we each contain energies of body, mind and spirit of which we must maintain equilibrium between all three energies. To preserve this balance we utilize our threefold powers. Use of mental, spiritual and physical powers in a spiritual way must produce abundance.
2. All thoughts begin with an idea which is the byproduct of divine connection to the source of all thought.
3. The ideas in back of the thought are the mystical form of all creation and the underpinnings of tangible results or manifestation.
4. All thoughts tend to lead to the field of potential outcomes for all actions, inactions, and creation.
5. Deep Thinking or what is believed in mind habitually becomes who you are and is your essence or character.
6. Free will creates Choices where commitments must be selected. We all have the ability to choose how we use free will in terms of thoughts and actions.
7. Choices create the nucleus of new form and begin a chain reaction if the choice is fueled with emotion and belief.
8. Emotions that fuel manifestation are love, joy, peace, happiness, goodness, and other positive emotions.
9. When each idea is transformed into a intention, then each intention may be transformed into a plan, vision, and mission. Then it is chosen as a prime objective for the individual

10.   When the plan is primus it becomes a purpose which is backed by belief.

11.   When firm belief, earnestness and constructive emotion are in back of a purpose, it is energized.

12.   Our belief system must be based on the constant and creative possibility of optimal results and prosperity. Everyone who is living upright in a spiritual way is deserving and capable of tapping into this abundance.

13.   We become best at co-creating our destiny when we are in spiritual unity with the universe where a person develops the realization of the Divine Presence within one's own self.

14.   We operate most effectively when we are awakened and clear in mind. Attunement and forgiveness of ourselves and others allows us to be free of anger and to live in the present moment fully in an awakened state of mind.

15.   Acceptance - We must believe that prosperity and well-being is our birthright.

16.   Believe that you have wealth and freedom and that you are the essence of creative ability.

17.   Everything that is needed is continually provided by an ever expanding world and universe that is abundant and impersonal.

18.   We must understand the essence or rationale behind the purpose of each desire that we want to cultivate.

19.   Further, we must comprehend in some way how our big ideas will help others along with ourselves to convey the sincere impression of value, worth, and increase.

20.   Before implementing each plan or taking any big step, we evaluate our mental effectiveness. Getting clear and going thought a catharsis of mind. This means to look at your track record, atone, prune, purge, and clear away the mental debris.

Begin to use "what works" and start to utilize the best practices which make you efficient.

21.   Clear Objectives - Set specific goals, research and refine them. After the purpose, task and objective is clear, then push forward with persistence.

22.   Results Driven.   What is the mission, destination, vision. Develop affirmations that correlate to the most favorable end-result.

23.   Think, feel and act "AS IF" you are already in possession of the life that you want. Cultivate your emotions and your character around the "As If". You must become what you want which means you become the person who owns the life you desire.

24.   Look at where you are, where you are going and periodically reset the course and navigation to optimize the journey.

25.   Learn to think and speak in a prosperous way that conveys peace, abundance, and increase. Mold the habits and tendencies of your thought. Refuse to accept lack and fear.

26.   Take action. Keep lists and do three things toward your dreams per day, do them constructively to the best of your ability.

27.   Study your life, reflect on your day, decide how to continually improve yourself. Do your homework and do all you can to learn and know your purpose, objectives and master your skills. Be the best at what you do and BE Known for your excellence.

28.   Meditations and Prayer - Write out affirmative meditations such as, "Each day I am improving". Write out 10 statements that are affirming and positive. Contemplate over them each day. You can write out generalized affirmations or very specific ones.

29.   Use the affirmative statements or contemplation, to increase acceptance of our potential and boost our awareness.

30.   Visualize - See yourself in optimal circumstances in your mind's eye and Feel it. If you can visualize the optimal result, then see the next step. Example. See yourself a few pounds leaner toward your optimal weight.

31.   Choose your environment. Select what to feed yourself. Mold your circumstances by your actions and specific thought.

32.   Organize your affairs. Gain the habit of finishing things well. Become excellence, simplify your life, empty the clutter, and redefine your focus. Develop prosperity based routines.

33.   Imprint and affirm your ideals and dreams into your consciousness. The plan, desired thing, or result must be written and then verbalized. It should be claimed into this world using the spoken word.

34.   Make wealth and excellence a priority. Align your thoughts to attract excellence and wealth. Be aware, be open, learn to receive from others, offer praise, and appreciate life. Accept your potentiality, gifts, and abundance.

35.   Circulate your GOOD. Service and Giving - Donate time or money to people or organizations who are the source of your spiritual sustenance.

36.   Sixth Sense - Learn and practice creativity, awareness, and contemplation. Keep a journal, write out ideas, develop and allow a universal flow of inspiration and ideas into your life.

37.   Review and remember your actions. Reflect on what you have done well each day and things you may not have excelled upon. Be determined to be better and do the right thing. Over 200 years ago, Ben Franklin worked his precepts of order each evening. He wanted to be excellent and build his character even at a mature age.

38.   Research ideas - What are your passions, how do your ideas serve? Listen to your intuition & cultivate strategy. Look at what it would take to implement or be successful with your new ideas: then act on them, implement the plan, review the plan and then improve it.

39.   List out streams of income and potential ways to serve and be prosperous. List how you will expand your life. Go past your comfort zones. List goals beyond your expectations and have deadlines of specificity. You can always change the date.

40.   Review your lists and projects. Check off your accomplishments.

41.   Meet with partners, family and/or spouse to define goals.

42.   Discover your natural expression. What is your labor of love. Where do your passions lie. Remember that you work to pay bills, but you should always follow your dreams. Devote 20 percent of your waking hours each week to your passion. If you become great at it, odds are you can earn a living doing it too.

43.   Character - How do you want to BE.? Self respect and self regard can be developed and nurtured. When you rebuild yourself, you will in-turn love yourself better which allows you to be kinder, more generous, and more loving to others.

44.   With Character comes responsibility toward your mental, physical and spiritual health. Do what works to take care of yourself with: diet, exercise, learning, sleep, study, and fellowship.

45.   Associate with those who can help you where you can also help them. Create a network of business and spiritual friends.

46.   Be good to yourself. Learn health self regard and cultivate a loving relationship with the Source.

47.   Teaching others - Giving it away to keep it.

48.   Law of Increase and Charisma - Radiate abundance, cheer and enthusiasm. Be contagious with love, cheer, and enthusiasm.

How to Get What You Want – Super Charge Your Mind

1. Consciousness & Mind has been described as the substance by which the soul is given the chance to experience existence in the physical world.
2. There is no greater service to humanity than to make the best of yourself.
3. YOU must get rid of the last vestige of the old idea that there is a Deity whose will it is that you should be poor, or whose purposes may be served by keeping you in poverty.
4. In order to know more, do more, and be more we must have more; we must have things to use, for we learn, and do, and

become, only by using things. We must get rich, so that we can live more.

5. To get rich, you need only to use your will power upon yourself.

6. Do not talk about poverty; do not investigate it, or concern yourself with it. Never mind what its causes are; you have nothing to do with them.

7. What concerns you is the cure. Use your will power to keep your mind OFF the subject of poverty, and to keep it fixed with faith and purpose ON the vision of what you want.

8. If your heart is set on domestic happiness, remember that love flourishes best where there is refinement, a high level of thought, and freedom from corrupting influences; and these are to be found only where riches are attained by the exercise of creative thought, without strife or rivalry.

9. Getting what you want is in the effective application of a cause

10.   The cause of success is always in the person who succeeds

11.   The key to success is finding the cause of success and replicating the cause.

12.   Use your strongest faculty, and you can cultivate any faculty

13.   Can I have to realize you are potential and empower you must use your faculties in your skills effectively

14.   You must learn to create conscious action.

15.   Cultivate Gratitude and Harmonious Mind

16.   Poise is the combination of peace and power that can be applied to each action or thought.

17.   Act in a Certain Way in all you do with effectiveness, efficiency and providing value or increase to all.

18.   Power consciousness is the secret to success. Power consciousness is what you feel when you know that you can do a thing and you KNOW exactly how to do it.

19.   Belief is the other key to mastery because you MUST believe that it is possible for you to achieve success, while you must believe that you can learn how to do something effectively and flawlessly.

20.   The more steady and continuous your faith and purpose, the more rapidly you will get rich, because you will make only POSITIVE impressions upon Substance; and you will not neutralize or offset them by negative impressions.

21.   The picture of your desires, held with faith and purpose, is taken up by the Formless, and permeates it to great distances-throughout the universe

22.   You must bring things from your conscious mind into your subconscious so that you will know instinctively how to do tasks. Truly knowing in your deeper mind is similar to when you drive a car and speak on the phone as your deeper mind is Knowingly and unconsciously guiding your driving.

23.   We must learn how to effectively send ideas, techniques, and plans from the idea phase in mind into our subconscious mind. We can use tools such as auto suggestion and making a picture board, or use incantations to imprint ideas onto our sub consciousness

24.   Learn to utilize your existing assets in the now

25.   Learn to affect the function of each task you engage

26.   Do all you can in the now and feel your present place in the now

27.   Make use of your present environment

28.   Form of a clear conception of which you see in your mind and on the picture screen of your mind

29.   You can phone clear conceptions of each task that needs to be achieved

30.   Become more successful by using constructively the business you have now

31.   We may secure more friends buy using constructively the network you already have

32.   We may achieve greater domestic happiness by the constructive use of the love that already exists in your home.

33.   You can get what you want in the future by concentrating all your energies upon the constructive use of whatever you are in relation with today and the NOW

34.   A surplus of life causes evolution, growth, and opportunity.

35.   Take an interest in all people you meet me the business of socially and since their leaders of the best for them. This will create the advancement for you

36.   Respect yourself the absolutely charged to all put life into every act and fought and fixed power consciousness fought up on the fact that you are entitled two big promotion it will come as soon as you can more than feel your present place in everyday

37.   Our you must be well rounded and balanced and body and mind and soul and in love.

38.   Focus on doing what must be done. Take action in areas that can be effective in your life.

39.   Whenever you find yourself hurrying, call a halt; fix your attention on the mental image of the thing you want, and begin to give thanks that you are getting it. The exercise of GRATITUDE will never fail to strengthen your faith and renew your purpose.

40.   Man may come into full harmony with the Formless Substance by entertaining a lively and sincere gratitude for the blessings it bestows upon him. Gratitude unifies the mind of man with the intelligence of Substance, so that man's thoughts are received by the Formless.

41.   Man must form a clear and definite mental image of the things he wishes to have, to do, or to become; and he must hold this mental image in his thoughts, while being deeply

grateful to the Supreme that all his desires are granted to him. The man who wishes to get rich must spend his leisure hours in contemplating his Vision, and in earnest thanksgiving that the reality is being given to him.

42.   Too much stress cannot be laid on the importance of frequent contemplation of the mental image, coupled with unwavering faith and devout gratitude. This is the process by which the impression is given to the Formless, and the creative forces set in motion.

43.   The whole matter turns on receiving, once you have clearly formed your vision. When you have formed it, it is well to make an oral statement, addressing the Supreme in reverent prayer; and from that moment you must, in mind, receive what you ask for.

44.   In order to receive his own when it shall come to him, man must be active And he must do, every day, all that can be done that day, taking care to do each act in a successful manner and he must so hold the Advancing Thought that the impression of increase will be communicated to all with whom he comes in contact.

- *There is a thinking substance from which all things are made, and which, in its original state, permeates, penetrates, and fills the interspaces of the universe.*

- *A thought, sent into this substance, Produces the thing that is imaged by the thought.*

- *Man can form things in his thought, and, by impressing his thought upon formless substance, can cause the thing he thinks about to be created.*

- *In order to do this, man must pass from the competitive to the creative mind; he must form a clear mental picture of the things he wants, and hold this picture in his thoughts with the fixed PURPOSE to get what he wants, and the unwavering FAITH that he does get what he wants, closing his mind to all that may tend to shake his purpose, dim his vision, or quench his faith.*

- *That he may receive what he wants when it comes, man must act NOW upon the people and things in his present environment.*

- *In order to do this, man must pass from the competitive to the creative mind; he must form a clear mental picture of the things he wants, and do, with faith and purpose, all that can be done each day, doing each separate thing in an efficient manner.*

- Man may come into full harmony with the Formless Substance by entertaining a lively and sincere gratitude for the blessings it bestows upon him. Gratitude unifies the mind of man with the intelligence of Substance, so that man's thoughts are received by the Formless.

- Man must form a clear and definite mental image of the things he wishes to have, to do, or to become; and he must hold this mental image in his thoughts, while being deeply grateful to the Supreme that all his desires are granted to him. The man who wishes to get rich must spend his leisure hours in contemplating his Vision, and in earnest thanksgiving that the reality is being given to him.

- In order to receive his own when it shall come to him, man must be active; and this activity can only consist in more than filling his present place. He must keep in mind the Purpose to get rich through the realization of his mental image. And he must do, every day, all that can be done that day, taking care to do each act in a successful manner. He must give to every man a use value in excess of the cash value he receives, so that each transaction makes for more life; and he must so hold the Advancing Thought that the impression of increase will be communicated to all with whom he comes in contact. [ix]

Quotes on Prosperity and Abundance

- **"Wealth is not his that has it, but his who enjoys it." — Benjamin Franklin**

- **"Life is a field of unlimited possibilities." —Deepak Chopra**

- "He who is plenteously provided for from within, needs but little from without." —Johann Wolfgang von Goethe

- "Take full account of the excellencies which you possess, and in gratitude remember how you would hanker after them, if you had them not." —Marcus Aurelius

- "Whenever anything negative happens to you, there is a deep lesson concealed within it, although you may not see it at the time." —Eckhart Tolle

- "If you want to change who you are, begin by changing the size of your dream. Even if you are broke, it does not cost you anything to dream of being rich. Many poor people are poor because they have given up on dreaming." —Robert Kiyosaki

- "Ideas are the beginning points of all fortunes." —Napoleon Hill

- "When you are grateful fear disappears and abundance appears." —Anthony Robbins

"Everything in the universe has a purpose. Indeed, the invisible intelligence that flows through everything in a purposeful fashion is also flowing through you." —Dr. Wayne Dyer

- "Gratitude is an attitude that hooks us up to our source of supply. And the more grateful you are, the closer you become to your maker, to the architect of the universe, to the spiritual core of your being. It's a phenomenal lesson." —Bob Proctor

- **"Living in Abundance and Success is a Reasonable Option" — Magus Incognito**

- **"You have a divine right to abundance, and if you are anything less than a millionaire, you haven't had your fair share." — Stuart Wilde**

- **"Prosperity is not just having things. It is the consciousness that attracts the things. Prosperity is a way of living and thinking, and not just having money or things. Poverty is a way of living and thinking, and not just a lack of money or things." —Eric Butterworth**

- **"Most folks are about as happy as they make up their minds to be." —Abraham Lincoln**

- *"And he shall be like a tree planted by the rivers of water, that bringeth forth his fruit in his season; his leaf also shall not wither; and whatsoever he doeth shall prosper." —Psalm 1:3*

- **"The Constitution only gives people the right to pursue happiness. You have to catch it yourself." —Benjamin Franklin**

- **"Not what we have But what we enjoy, constitutes our abundance." — Epicurus**

- **"Gratitude is the vital ingredient in the recipe for Faith" — Magus Incognito**

- **"We may divide thinkers into those who think for themselves and those who think through others. The latter are the rule and** the former the exception. The first are original thinkers in a double sense, and egotists in the noblest meaning of the word." —Arthur Schopenhauer

- "The key to every man is his thought. Sturdy and defiant though he look he has a helm which he obeys, which is the idea after which all his facts are classified. He can only be reformed by showing him a new idea which commands his own." —Ralph Waldo Emerson

- "All truly wise thoughts have been thought already thousands of times; but to make them really ours we must think them over again honestly till they take root in our personal expression." — Johann Wolfgang von Goethe.

- "Great men are they who see that spirituality is stronger than any material force; that thoughts rule the world." —Ralph Waldo Emerson.

- "All that we are is a result of what we have thought." —Buddha

- "Wealth is the slave of a wise man. The master of a fool." — Seneca

- "Happiness is not in the mere possession of money; it lies in the joy of achievement, in the thrill of creative effort." — Franklin D Roosevelt

- "Money is like manure. You have to spread it around or it smells." — J. Paul Getty

- "Liberty is not a means to a higher political end. It is the highest political end." — Lord John Dalberg-Acton

- "We are what we repeatedly do. Excellence, then, is not an act but a habit." —Aristotle

- "Money is like love; it kills slowly and painfully the one who withholds it, and enlivens the other who turns it on his fellow man." — Kahlil Gibran

- "Empty pockets never held anyone back. Only empty heads and empty hearts can do that." —Norman Vincent Peale

- "The thief cometh not, but for to steal, and to kill, and to destroy: I am come that they might have life, and that they might have it more abundantly." —John 10:10, KJV

- "Prosperity is not without many fears and distastes, and adversity is not without comforts and hopes." —Francis Bacon

- "It is health that is real wealth and not pieces of gold and silver." — Mahatma Gandhi

- "Desire is the starting point of all achievement, not a hope, not a wish, but a keen pulsating desire, which transcends everything. When your desires are strong enough you will appear to possess superhuman powers to achieve."— Napoleon Hill

- "Move out of your comfort zone. You can only grow if you are willing to feel awkward and uncomfortable when you try something new." — Brian Tracy

- "You can open your mind to prosperity when you realize the true definition of the word: You are prosperous to the degree you are experiencing peace, health and plenty in your world." —Catherine Ponder, *Open Your Mind to Prosperity*

- "There is a science of getting rich and it is an exact science, like algebra or arithmetic. There are certain laws which govern the process of acquiring riches and once these laws are learned and obeyed by anyone, that person will get rich with mathematical certainty." —*Wallace D. Wattles*

- "Within you right now is the power to do things you never dreamed possible. This power becomes available to you just as soon as you can change your beliefs." —*Dr. Maxwell Maltz*

Appendix - A Concise Chronology of Esoteric Spirituality

Here is a basic timetable of Esoteric Spirituality and Gnosticism

1. Zarathustra 1000-1500 BC Persia

2. Heraclitus – 6th Century BC

3. Pythagoras – Born 571 BC Century BC Greece – Italy

4. Laozi – Lao Tzu – Taoism Born 571 BC

5. Confucius Born 551 BC

6. Siddhartha Gautama (Buddhism) – 6th Century BC India

7. Socrates, Plato, Aristotle - 4th Century BC

8. Epicurus – 3rd Century BC

9. Cicero 40 BC

10.	Marcus Aurelius 180 AD

11.	Iamblichus 300 AD

12.	St. Benedict 5th Century

13.	Scottus Johannes Erigena – 9th Century

14.	Hildegard von Bingen – 11th Century

15.	Meister Eckhart 13th Century Mystic

16.	Hus – Jacob Boheme – Moravian Piety

17.	Rosicrucians – 14th Century

18.	Martin Luther – 16th Century

19.   Baruch Spinoza - 1632 – 1677

20.   von Zinzendorf und Pottendorf

21.   Liebniz 1710

22.   Hegel 1807

23.   Schopenhauer 1818

24.   Emerson and Thoreau 1860s – American Transcendentalism

25.   Theosophical Groups 1875 to present.

26.   Judge Thomas Troward 1900

27.   Carl Jung – Gnostic Mysticism

28.   Dr. Samuel M Shoemaker – Oxford Movement 1900-1940s

29.   Heȟáka Sápa, commonly known as Black Elk 1863-1950

30.   12 Step Programs – 1930s

31.   21st Century – Wayne Dyer – Eckhart Tolle – The Secret Speakers

Many more people could be included in this chronology as this is a short and generalized list.

About the Author George Mentz –

Commissioner George Mentz JD MBA CWM Chartered Wealth Manager ® is an international book award winning author, award winning professor, licensed attorney and CEO of GAFM ® global education. Mentz has been recognized as the #2 in the world as a Wealth Management influencer and his Wealth Management Handbook has reached the top 75 Wealth books in History. Mentz's education companies are ISO 21001 and ISO 9001 Certified professional development companies offering wealth management training & operating in over 50 nations. Mentz is an advisory board member to several companies around the world in education, charities, and FinTech Companies.   Mentz holds a Doctor of Jurisprudence degree, and MBA, and a Graduate International Law Diploma/Certificate along with federal and state law licenses. Mentz is an Associate of The St. George's House, Windsor Castle, UK. Mentz and his companies have been seen in The Hill, The Wall Street Journal, The Week UK, The Hindu, the El Norte Mexico, Magazine of Wall Street, Newsmax, The China Daily, ABC,NBC, CBS, FOX, The Arab Times, and many more.   Mentz is the titular Lord/Seigneur of the Fief Blondel Est. 1270 AD and a titular Lord of Annaly. All Rights Reserved 2021

Other References or Authors of Interest

Allen, J. (1998). *As You Think*. Edited with an introduction by M. Allen. Novato, CA: New World Library.

Aurelius, M. (1964) *Meditations*, trans. M. Staniforth, London: Penguin.

The Bhagavad-Gita (1973) trans. J. Mascaró, London: Penguin World's Classics..

Behrend, G. (1927) *Your Invisible Power*. Montana: Kessinger Publishing.

Carnegie, D. (1994). *How to Win Friends and Influence People*. New York: Pocket Books.

Carlson, R. (2001). *Don't Sweat the Small Stuff About Money*. New York, USA: Hyperion.

Chopra, D. (1996). *The Seven Spiritual Laws of Success*. London: Bantam Press.

Collier, R. (1970). *Be Rich*. Oak Harbor, Washington: Robert Collier Publishing.

Coelho, P. (1999) *The Alchemist*, trans. Alan R Clarke, London: HarperCollins.

Covey, S. R. (1989). *The 7 Habits of Highly Effective People*. London: Simon & Schuster.

Dyer, W. (1993). *Real Magic: Creating Miracles in Everyday Life.* New York: HarperCollins.

Eker, T. H. (2005). *Secrets of the Millionaire Mind: Mastering the Inner Game of Wealth.* New York: HarperCollins Publishers.

Emerson, R.W. (1993) *Self-Reliance,* Dover Publications.

Gawain, Shakti (1979). *Creative Visualization.* New World Library, Mill Valley USA.

Bishop Bernard Jordan (2007). The Laws of Thinking: 20 Secrets to Using the Divine Power of Your Mind to Manifest Prosperity." (2007) *(9781401917968): Published by Hay House and Bishop E. Bernard Jordan: Books*

Hill, N. (1960). *Think and Grow Rich.* New York: Fawcett Crest.

His Holiness the Dalai Lama, with H. C. Cutler (1999). *The Art of Happiness: A Handbook for Living.* London: Hodder & Stroughton.

James, W. (1902). *The Varieties of Religious Experience.* Longman Publishing, London, UK.

Jeffers, S. (1991) Feel the Fear and Do It Anyway, London: Arrow Books.

Lao-Tzu's Tao Te Ching (2000) trans. T. Freke, introduction by M.

Palmer, London: Piatkus.

Maltz, M.. (1960). *Psycho-Cybernetics.* New York. Pocket Books.

Marden, O. S. (1997). *Pushing to the Front, or Success under Difficulties,* Vols. 1–2. Santa Fe, California: Sun Books.

Mentz, C. W. H. (2007). *Masters of the Secrets: And the Science of Getting Rich and Master Key System Expanded: Bestseller Version.* Bloomington, Indiana, United States: Xlibris Corp.

Mentz, C. W. H. (2006). *How to Master Abundance and Prosperity— The Master Key System Decoded.* Bloomington Indiana: Xlibris Pub.

Mentz, C. W. H. (2005). *The Science of Growing Rich.* Bloomington, Indiana: Xlibris Publishing.

Mentz, George S - *Other Books by Mentz.* http://www.lulu.com/gmentz

Mulford, P. (1908). *Thoughts Are Things: Essays Selected from the White Cross Library.* G. Bell and Sons, Ltd., LONDON, 1908.

Murphy, J. (1963). *The Power of Your Subconscious Mind.* New Jersey: Prentice Hall.

Peale, N.V. (1996) *The Power of Positive Thinking*, New York: Ballantine Books.

Ponder, C. (1962). *The Dynamic Laws of Prosperity.* Camarillo, California: DeVorss & Co.

Price, J. R. (1987). *The Abundance Book.* Carlsbad, California: Hay House.

Roman, S., Packer, D. R. (2008). Creating Money: *Attracting Abundance.* Tiburon, California: H. J. Kramer, Inc., published in a joint venture with New World Library.

Scovell Shinn, F. (1998) *The Game of Life and How to Play It*, Saffron

Walden: C.W. Daniel.

Seicho-no Iye (生長の家). Books by Dr. Masaharu Taniguchi.

Smiles, S. (2002). *Self-Help: With Illustrations of Character, Conduct, and Perseverance.* Oxford: Oxford University Press.

Thoreau, H.D. (1986) *Walden and Civil Disobedience*, introduction by M. Meyer, New York: Penguin.

Tracy, B. (1993). *Maximum Achievement: Strategies and Skills That Will Unlock Your Hidden Powers to Succeed.* New York: Fireside.

Troward, T. (1904). *The Edinburgh Lectures on Mental Science.* DODD, MEAD & COMPANY: New York.

Wattles, W. D. (1976). *Financial Success through the Power of Thought: The Science of Getting Rich.* Rochester, Vermont: Destiny Books.

Wilkinson, B. (2000). *The Prayer of Jabez.* Colorado Springs, CO USA, OR: Multnamah Publishers.

[i] Pg. 160 The American Journal of Sociology, Volume 72 Albion Woodbury Small, Ellsworth Faris, Ernest Watson Burgess University of Chicago Press, 1895 - Social sciences

[ii] Architectural Record - Volume 155 - Page 65 - McGraw-Hill, 1891 - Architecture
https://books.google.com › books

[iii] W. D. Wattles enhanced by Prof. Mentz from "Financial Success Through Creative Thought " 1910

[iv] W.D. Wattles - How to Be a Genius 1911

[v] "The Science of Being Great" by Wattles – Elizabeth Towne Publishing 1914

[vi] I W. D. Wattles enhanced by Prof. Mentz from "Financial Success Through Creative Thought " 1910

[vii] W.D. Wattles - IBID

[viii] **Lifespring**: Getting Yourself from Where You Are to Where You Want to Be by John Hanley - 1989

[ix] Wattles, W. D. (1976). *Financial Success through the Power of Thought: The Science of Getting Rich.* Rochester, Vermont: Destiny Books.